# APRIL FLOWERS

## MELANIE ALLEN

# Contents

# Prologue: Planting Seeds

Grinning from ear to ear. My little boy lays there sleeping on the couch. Something in his slumber has him grinning from ear to ear. I watch him sleeping, laying on his side with one chubby foot in my lap, the leg underneath bent at the knee and his chubby hands folded in prayer under his cheek. He wanted to watch Spider-Man again, but he fell asleep, and I sit here watching the rest of it by myself. When he wakes up in the morning, I know he will ask to turn it on again because he didn't get to finish it when he fell asleep. So, I'll have to watch the whole thing again. A million times for him, a trillion times for me. Because I'm his Mama, that's what I do for this little stinker. He is sleeping so hard. He does some silent giggling in his sleep, still smiling off and on, his breath and throat feigning a belly laugh while his body jerks up and down with a few quick giggles out loud. Every mom wants a happy, healthy kid and laying here beside me, I have one. Just looking at him makes me grin from ear to ear myself. A fresh haircut makes him look more boy than baby. At 3 now, he is somewhere in between acting like he's ready to drive a car but still has mom helping him climb the playground set at the park to get to his favorite slide. We had a long day and spent hours at the park. Climbing, running, sliding, swinging, and eventually stomping on green Tootsie-Roll sized goose poop on the sidewalk on purpose. Then it was time to go.

He showered head to toe in green apple scented hair and body wash. He's wearing his Spider-Man pajamas grinning from ear to ear while I watch his movie. I don't want to move. I don't want to move him. So, we will sleep on the couch. Why not? Before he went to sleep, he practiced all his new kisses he learned. He gave me an "England kiss," one on each cheek. Then, he said next was an "Eskimo kiss," where he rubbed the tip of his nose on mine probably a lot harder than it is supposed to be. Then the next one was a "butterfly kiss," when he got his eye real close to my cheek and blinked really hard to brush my cheek lightly with his eyelashes, although he never does anything lightly. And the new one he learned was to "blow me a kiss." So, he kissed his chubby little hand, outstretched his hand and blew it to me. He said, "Moooooooom! You're supposed to catch it!" I replied, "Oh, sorry, do it again and I'll catch it this time." So, he repeated the kiss on his hand and blows it to me. This time I caught it with both hands, take my one hand with the kiss still in my fist and put it on my cheek lovingly and said, "Thank you." Harley said, "No, no, no, no! Not like that. You blow a kiss to me, and I'll show you what to do." So, I comply with his orders. I kissed my palm and blew it to him. He caught it by slapping his hands in front of him and cupped his hands like he's holding it. He swung his cupped hands over both shoulders and shook it up like he just won a prize fight, and slapped one hand over his mouth throwing the kiss in. He proceeded to fake chew it up and exaggerates swallowing it. He put his tongue between his lips and made a fake fart sound. He lifted and said, "I blew you a kiss." That's my sweet little boy. Corrupted by older sisters. He gets funnier every day. We both laugh, and I roll my eyes a little as he over announces his laugh with, "Ha. Ha. Ha."

And when I ask him what he wants to watch knowing it's going to be Spider-Man, I act surprised and put it on for him knowing I'll be finishing it by myself. He's worth it. I snuggle in behind him on the couch to finish the movie. If my heart could smile, it was doing it right now, from ear to ear. Like Spider-Man, I too have a great responsibility. These kids aren't going to raise themselves. I think about being a mom and the responsibility that comes with it. Do you take what you know and pass it down? Read books? Trial and error? Fake it? Wing it? Get creative and make it up as you go? Mix and match what works for each kid? It's a crazy thought being responsible for another human and having a hand in what they do or don't become. A great responsibility. Yes, indeed.

My baby boy Harley just turned 3 and he has me thinking. Really thinking with my soul and not my head or heart. Deep thoughts of a Hard Knocks Mama. I don't need stuff or things or crafts or flowers. I just want my children to be the little cleaning ladies around the house that I always dreamed they would be; doing dishes, vacuum, mow the lawn, clean the house, do the laundry, etc., even for just one day. I am not a fancy person. I don't need fancy things. I'm more than happy to bend over backwards to do anything for each and every one of them. It is what I do. I have a great responsibility. But the road to this snuggle on the couch with this green apple-smelling, fake farting little boy wasn't a straight path. It was a journey for myself as a freckle-faced, half-Mexican girl on a winding road with twists and turns of fate, confusion, chaos, and dumb shit that made me who I am today. At times my road was a muddy mess, and I was lost. At times my road was a highway and I'm moving too fast and going too far. But these days my road is a country road. No one in front of me. No one behind me. I can drive as fast or as slow as I want. And I do. And I take my time to get there. This life we live can be an adventure. Depends on how you look at it. What might break one down, only makes another stronger. There is no rhyme or reason to it.

Have you ever heard the saying "April showers brings May flowers?" The saying means you must endure the rain to find a beautiful ending. Or the beautiful whatever's next. Sometimes I feel that is the theme of my life. Except between the rain and the beautiful, lies heartache and hardship. Rain can be cold, and unforgiving; a painful relentless destroyer. Rain can be refreshing, cleansing, and satisfying. Just like life. I feel as though the beautiful outcome from the rain is just as beautiful as the dance in the rain to get there. I am the springtime. I am the struggle. I am the outcome of that struggle. I am new life starting over. I don't follow the rules. I don't like being told how to do things. I have given myself a path to follow. I have endured the pain of the rain. I have endured a life full of ups and downs in between the showers and the flowers. I am in the beginning and the middle and always working towards a beautiful ending.

Consider what it means to grow a flower. You plant the seed, and it grows. The End. But we also need to nurture it. It needs sunlight. And we need to water it. It needs some attention to make sure it grows up strong. Sometimes no matter where you plant the seed, it grows. Some people believe there are bad seeds. No one really knows if that is true. Some plants thrive despite the lack of water because the rain naturally comes anyway. Some thrive despite the lack of sunshine because the daylight is just enough light to keep it growing. And some thrive despite the lack of attention because the other little plants surrounding the flower keep it company.  Some just grow, and it's a miracle of nature. Some never grow to reach their full potential. Some just barely make it.  They look like all the other flowers, but they are just a little smaller.  And some wither up.   Raising little humans is the same way. With the proper water and sunlight, some still wither. Without the proper water and sunlight, some still flower. That is a perfect description of who I am.

# CHAPTER ONE

# The Blizzard

Where I come from, pre-dates me. I came to be because my parents came to be and their parents and so on. So, I come from my mother's family in Mexico. And my father's family in West Virginia. And because these two connected, is why I'm here. I'm a mongrul, a mutt, a mixed-breed, a Mexi-billy with Brack hair (not quite black but darker than brown). I have my mother's dark eyes, high cheek bones (hidden under my face fat), and my mother's dimples. Well, she has dimples, I have a dimple. I have one dimple and a half dimple. We call that one a himple. I have my father's freckles. I didn't grow up speaking Spanish, although my mother is fluent. I speak the language of my father; Profanity. I am fluent as well. I will do my best to spell out exactly how April Flowers came to be. As I suddenly found myself closer and closer to 50, the fear began to set in that as I age, I will lose my memories, my stories, and that bull shit I made up along the way will overrun the real parts of my life that I can't really truly remember. But I remember enough to know my story, my life, and how I came to be is a pretty fun thing to talk about. I figure, I may as well write about it too. This isn't a self-help book. I think of it more as a parenting book, but exactly what not to do. It is a cautionary tale of resiliency.

I do recognize I have had some horrid shit happen in my life, but most people have. It makes me less surprised when more horrid shit happens. Therefore, those who haven't had to deal with the drama and trauma as I have come to know as normal life, become paralyzed and unable to handle it when it happens. I laugh at shit that isn't funny because I have a disgustingly morbid sense of humor. But don't mistake me for cruel or rude. I laugh because I have to, or I would crumble under the weight of chaos. I joke and make fun and find the light side of the darkness. It's how I survive. It's how I have flourished and survived. I need those giggles. I am a true Mexi-billy. I can laugh at myself, therefore, expect that I for sure will laugh at others.

My Mexican side of the family hails from South of the American border, not a Texas Mexican, a real-life Mexican. My mother, Dreama, was born in Mexico. She never knew or met her father. Or at least that was the story we have been told. Her mother went on to have other children with another man and my mother became an outcast. From the way she always told us kids, she was very much hated by her siblings and her mother. She didn't belong in her family and was treated very cruelly from a very young age. She suffered extreme physical abuse, and my grandmother even whacked her ankle with a hammer when she was a little girl. She was kicked out of her home by the age of 10. She had a tumultuous relationship with her mother and her half-siblings. There was always undertones of resentment and jealousy, along with mistrust of one another. Based on there being no relationship with her siblings, I was never able to know or love that part of my family. When you are a child, life just appears before you.

It is given to you, and you just go about your days none-the-wiser and live it. That's what we are handed. But as an adult, it is sad to know and understand an entire half of who I am is out there somewhere. I wonder if I look like any of them. I wonder if they laugh like me. I wonder if they know about me and wonder the same things about me. I wonder if they too have a himple. It is that sense of wonder that hangs over your thoughts to seek out answers to what is not known. To me, in my field of work, that is the undertone of why I have found more children adopted as infants seek out their birth families. While they wonder and fantasize about who they are and what they are, there is a natural, animal instinct to find answers, to fill the holes in your sense of knowing who you are and where you belong. Children who are adopted when they are older or who have the answers provided to them, openly discussed and shared stories of their biological family, as much as the adoptive families are aware of, help those adopted children fill their sense of belonging without questions, without wonder, and with those answers already available. There is much less desire to fill the holes in your sense of knowing who you are and where you belong.

According to Dreama, she never felt she belonged anywhere or to anyone. She lived on the streets of Mexico for a while until some nuns in a convent took pity on her and took her in. She only went to school to the 6$^{th}$ grade. She panhandled and scrounged for cans to sell to have a little bit of money. She also had to eat food from dumpsters or beg for scraps. She was finally taken in by her maternal Aunt and brought to the United States. Her maternal Aunt, my great Aunt TiTi and Uncle William could not have children. I suspect it is because my great Aunt was a teen prostitute in Mexico. Aunt TiTi was taken in by my great Uncle and they had a wonderful life together. However, it was a childless marriage. He was a businessman and they resided in Chicago.

They are the only Mexican side of the family I had the privilege to love. They had plenty of money and desired to take my mama into their home. Aunt TiTi and Uncle William became the parents my mother never had. They loved her and she loved them. Uncle William was a huge, ginormous man whose size could fill a doorway and his booming voice and laughter could fill an auditorium, with a deep rumble. And he had stories to tell. Well, apparently so do I.

Uncle William told tall tales of mystery and many stories about the ladies. No one was ever sure what to believe. We were never sure if his stories were true or not. And that was also the best part about listening to his stories. He would tell a tall tale about the bombing of Pearl Harbor with claims that he was there, and we were never able to verify if he was or not, but we loved hearing him go on. He was a sailor in the Navy and was enlisted during WWII. We were able to verify all of that through his paperwork and the photos of his Naval Academy class. He was one of the tallest ones and was super handsome in his uniform. He always loved to show us the tattoo on his arm of a lady in a hula skirt. He would wiggle it and make her dance. One of his stories about Pearl Harbor was about one of his friends. He claims during the bombing, his friend had his legs blown off and asked Uncle William to please end his life. He would talk about the booms. The yelling. The screaming. The pain. And the chaos. We were never sure if it was the tequila talking, if it was real, or if he was like me (or maybe I was like him) and he made up stories to cover the real ones that are often more painful. If that is the case, I hate to think of what he really saw that day.

He would sing us loud and boisterous sailor songs and would always end up teary-eyed and sobbing. Uncle William also lost his older brother, Bert, on the veteran patroller submarine, the USS Trout. This vessel left Pearl Harbor on February 8, 1944, enroute to her 11th patrol.

She topped off with fuel at Midway and left February 16th, never to be heard from again.  At the end of February, Sakito Maru was sunk and another ship badly damaged.  Since the USS Trout was the only U.S. submarine which could have attacked at that time and location, it is assumed she was lost during or shortly after these battles.  A crew of 81 were lost at sea, presumed missing and later declared KIA.  These two "men" at the ages of 18 and 19 are a part of the definition of the ultimate sacrifice.  For his service, Bert's family received a Purple Heart.  For the rest of us, our Freedom.

Uncle William loved to drink tequila.  He could and sometimes often did drink a fifth of Tequila a day.  He was often able to start a new bottle, as well.  His laugh and his stories would get louder and louder.  He liked the expensive tequila. He quite literally would cuss like a sailor, and I loved every minute of it.   This could also be the reason I am so great at profanity.  Aunt TiTi was a little eccentric to say the least.  She was always wearing a flowery dress with a puff of black fluffy bangs curled back high on her head and short hair.  She had a very quiet nature and the cutest giggle.  She would always say, "Oh Willy" and throw her hands in the air at him when he would get carried away drinking, cussing, and telling stories.  Aunt TiTi spoke with a high shrill voice and a thick Mexican accent.  Uncle William was not Mexican, but he was pretty fluent in Spanish. Aunt TiTi was super short, standing just under 5' tall.  Uncle William was over a foot and a half taller than her, and they made a cute couple of opposites.  They fawned all over the kids all of the time.  They loved to bring gifts when we were little.  They were the best kind, as we didn't have much.  My great aunt and uncle raised my mother as a pre-teen until she was around 18 years old when she met my father.  They were not too fond of him!

My mother was also pretty short, barely reaching 5'1". She has beautiful, thick, wavy black hair and always wore it very long. Down to her butt at times. She has the same thick Mexican accent as Aunt TiTi. She wore her nails too long and wore way too much eye liner. She has beautiful brown skin, high chiseled cheek bones, and such cute little dimples. She has dark brown eyes, and she always smelled like cocoa butter, stale liquor, and cigarettes. She drank liquor often. Little shots here and there. And some in her coffee. It is probably likely that her quick, evil temper erupted from too much alcohol and too many noisy children. She was quick with a belt and was not an affectionate mother. As kids, we had to mother ourselves. Or we found a mother substitute. This recurring theme has endured my whole life.

My dad's side of the family has its own interesting twists and turns, just like the country roads. My grandfather was the oldest of 6 and grew up in the coal mine area of West Virginia. Grandfather Merle, and my grandmother, Rose, also had 6 children. My dad was the baby of the family. Even later in life when we found a 7th child of Grandpa Merle's, my new aunt was just 7 months older than my father, meaning he was still the baby. My new Aunt Gertie was the spitting image of my oldest aunt. It was uncanny. My grandfather served in the military and was quite the ladies' man, per the many stories Grandma would talk about beating the ladies off of him with a stick when she was younger. Grandma Rose told us a story about following Grandpa Merle to the movies and sitting behind him and another woman at the theatre. Grandma Rose pulled her hair from behind and started a fight that ended up on the street. She told us she was on top of this woman hitting her and grabbed a brick from the street. She caught herself holding this brick up over her head ready to slam it in this woman's face. She suddenly caught herself and realized what she was about to do. And it scared her. She put the brick down and got up and walked off. She knew in that moment that she was driven to the brink of jealous rage, and she stopped herself.

Eventually once we found our new aunt, it just proved what everyone in town knew. Apparently, all the cousins went to school with Gertie, and there was talk of her, but no one ever came right out and said it until many, many years later. But for us we always say, the more the merrier. I loved the idea of having more people to add to my dad's side of the family due to the complete lack on my mother's side. My grandfather Merle died at the age of 49, and without knowing full details, according to family, he died from a stroke. My dad, Lanny Sr. was barely an adult when his father died. He was a chubby kid, and he liked to drink and play music. He and my mother met when she was 18 (he was 20), and within a year they were married and headed back to Ohio. My mama was desperate to get out from under her aunt and uncle's rule, and this seemed to be the perfect way.

Ohio is where much of Grandma Rose's family resided, in-laws, relatives, cousins, and relatives by marriage. Hell, this family was from West Virginia, they were sometimes married to each other AND related to each other! Yes, there's some of that in there. Mom's stories and accounting of history is hard to follow. Her time frames seem off, and she tends to blend stories together. She is also older now, so she remembers a lot of things out of order which is also very confusing. But, overall, even if 1% of the shit she endured was real or true, it is horrifying!

My parents wasted very little time and had my oldest brother in 1969, Lanny Jr. and the next child 11 months later in 1970, Andrew. My father played music and did side jobs for construction companies my whole life. In 1972, my sister Lola was born. She is the only one born in another state. They were visiting my dad's older brother Dale and his family in Maryland. So that was where Lola was born. A year later, the greatest human being that ever walked the face of the earth was born, mwah (how the hell do you spell that? Isn't mwah - a kiss sound?). Then the baby of our family, Christian, was born in 1975. That's a lot of kids for a young mom and dad. That's a lot of responsibility having 5 children in the span of 6 years. Some may actually say a bit of irresponsibility. If it seems like a recipe for disaster, it was.

According to my mother, my father also had a wandering eye. Like father, like son. She tells many stories of taking herself to the hospital and having babies alone while my father was off to God-knows-where. She also had to take a taxi home with Andrew because my dad never showed up at all after she had him in the hospital. She said she would drive herself, or sometimes a friend, or a neighbor took her. She didn't have any stories about our child births, just that she endured it all alone. We knew what hospital we were born in and where we were born, but never had any kind of story about the importance of us being born. No idea of deliveries, labor, nothing. It was almost like it wasn't important. Maybe it really wasn't.

Just a few short months after baby Christian was born, something God-awful happened that changed my mother and father forever. One summer, the 4th of July celebration was going on in our little Bellevue town. With all 5 kids in tow, mom was headed up to the park to hang out for some games and food and later, the fireworks. My mother has only told us this story in bits and pieces. And my dad never spoke a word of it. According to Dreama, she and all the kids were all walking behind the parked cars to head into the park for the festivities. There were family activities and baseball games. While she pushed a stroller, held hands with a toddler, and held a baby; the two boys, Lanny and Andrew, walked behind. They were 6 and 5 at the time. They walked up the tree-lined little street to get to the park entrance. Cars were parked along one side of the street facing into the park and it was bustling with everyone in town ready to celebrate and watching all of the baseball games that were going on. Lanny Jr. was charged with holding hands with Andrew. Andrew kept stopping to pick up rocks and throw them down the storm drain behind the cars. Lanny just happened to be just a few steps ahead before he realized Andrew had stopped again. Simultaneously, as he turns to tell Andrew to hurry, a car starts backing up. Not seeing the small kids walking behind his car, the 16-year-old teenager who just finished playing a baseball game, backed his car over a little boy, my brother Andrew.

My mother says she screamed, everyone else started yelling, and the teenage driver, not knowing what to do and in a panic, then went forward and ran over my brother again. My mother ran over to where Andrew was laying in the street and picked up her son's limp body. She opened the teenager's car door and jumped into the back seat of his car. Wailing, desperate for help for her son, she demanded the teenager take her to the hospital. To this very day I am not even sure my father was present when this incident happened, and she never talked about who took care of us kids when she took off with Andrew to the hospital. The local hospital was just a block away around the corner from the park. The teenager was sobbing uncontrollably, asking if he was ok, pleading with him to please be ok. Begging God to please let him be ok. He was crying so hard he was shaking as he drove this strange woman and the little boy he just ran over to the hospital. She said Andrew was looking up at her with his eyes wide and scared. He didn't make a sound, but tears were falling from his eyes. She could hardly bear to look at him as his little head began to already show signs of extreme swelling. She just held him in her lap for what seemed an eternity watching the life in his eyes slowly fade. He managed to say two words, in almost a whisper, "It hurts." And his breathing slowed. His blinks got slower and slower, and stopped. And her heart thumped with pain as she sobbed watching his lifeless body fall asleep right before her eyes. Even after 40 years, the anguish and heartache shows all over her face when she tells bits and pieces from that terrible day. It is a hurt so painful, welling up the thickest tears you will ever see. Just hearing her tell the story causes your heart to feel physical pain and angst trying to hold in your own tears. Andrew closed his eyes. Forever. No matter how quickly Andrew made it to the hospital, he died the next day.

My mother has never visited my brother's grave. As a poor family, my brother never had a head stone and to this day, he still does not have one. For nearly 40 years, there was literally nothing to show where his grave was until we asked the church and funeral home to verify where he was buried. The funeral home put a little marker at the head of his burial site. He is buried at a small cemetery of a very small church just outside of Clyde, the next town over. My grandma Rose's younger sister is also buried there. I suspect this is why my parents chose this place for him as well. Where this beloved child is buried has only a little silver flag marker that says "A. Allen". Burying my brother at the age of 5 destroyed my mother for nearly a year and broke her in pieces forever. It put a hurt on her heart for the rest of her life, and she still bears that pain when asked about it or when talking about it; as if it just happened yesterday. The image of his little face laying in her lap is something she will never forget. It is there when she closes her eyes. That image is something no mother should ever have to see. The image of pure heart break.

Andrew's life and his memory was reduced to mementos in a shoe box. A photograph of Andrew and Lanny with their arms draped over each other's shoulders, grinning from ear to ear wearing matching brown shorts, no shirts, and tall socks with a thick blue stripe at the top. Andrew and Lanny sitting next to each other in barber chairs with Andrew's light brown bangs hanging straight and bluntly across his forehead with his hair cape on. A yellow matchbox car. A baby shoe. A striped t-shirt. And a paper envelope with clippings of his hair from his first haircut. She would wander outside with his box of things and cry. My dad would tell her to get over it, take care of the kids she still had, and stop dwelling. He did so many evil things to crush my mom, and this nearly crushed her mind and soul. She said she had a difficult time thinking about the future and couldn't get his little face passing away right before her eyes of out her mind. She cries over Andrew with a truly broken heart. My father accused her of having an affair, and she tells us that he was almost indignant over his death. He never thought Andrew was his child. Ironically, he was the child that resembled my father the most, and who my own son takes after in appearance.

I cannot imagine the heart ache. I cannot imagine the pain my mother endured. My father was an SOB. My mother said he would hide Andrew's box from her and tease her. He would tell her he was tired of her crying and neglecting the home she still had and the children she still had to care for. He would hide the box in different places, and she would thrash all over the house looking for it in the oven, fridge, closet, cupboards, etc. He would call her a crazy psycho as he watched her hunt for the box, sometimes giving her clues and sometimes letting her know if she was hot or cold. Until one day, she searched and searched but was never able to find the box. Andrew's box of things disappeared for good. My father got rid of it and my mom has still never gotten over Andrew's death. She still blames herself for not having a hold of his hand. She blames herself for marrying my dad in the first place.  She blames herself and continues to carry that burden in her heart like Andrew's lost little box.

We lived in a little ranch house just outside of a super small town called Bellevue.  This area of Ohio and this town were known for manufacturing, and everyone's mom and aunt and grandma worked at the factory called General Electric.  We had a dog named Buffy. My dad played bass guitar and loved country music.  My dad had an uncle (my grandma Rose's brother) who was in the music business.  My dad looked up to him and loved to talk music and play music together. My great Uncle actually co-wrote a song with John Conlee for his first single and title track of his debut album, *Rose Colored Glasses*.  The song was released in 1978 and peaked at #5 on the charts.  He was so proud of this record.  He sent the family a 45 record of the single saying it was going to go to number one.  My great Uncle was a road manager for this country artist.  After one of their shows in California in 1984, he was struck and killed by a drunk driver as he guided the country singer's tour bus out of a parking lot. That was a huge blow to grandma, and his family was devastated.  My grandma Rose, my dad, and all of us kids were huge fans of John Conlee. We played his records every chance we got and loved all of his songs. We knew every song by heart.  They were the theme songs of my childhood about heartache, divorce, and having a new outlook on life.  Looking at life through rose-colored glasses never did us much good.  We were always just on the brink of something terrible no matter how you looked at it. We were too young to know about the things we knew about and to see the things we have seen.  Somehow, life was still beautiful, rosy, and perfect in so many ways, because we were still together and reveled in the good times we had.  Talk about resiliency!  We sure did need that.

1978 was also the same year Ohio was hit with a terrible, terrible Blizzard.  Nearly twelve inches of new snow fell on top of the already sixteen inches on the ground, totaling a shit ton of snow. Temperatures dropped into the teens and the 40 mph winds blew the snow all over. The snow drift in front of our little ranch-style house reached nearly as high as the roof! Our family's home was just outside of town, and the conditions were not pretty. Needless to say, I barely survived the blizzard of '78 without frostbite! We lost power for several days. It was fun at first camping out in the living room and the snow was as far as we could see. Eventually, we all ended up at the neighbor's house with their 3 children, since we were out of food. In what seems like just one sitting, we had gobbled up every bit of canned goods the neighbor mom had stored in her canning closet. We had two families sleeping in their living room to stay warm. But things took a turn when we ran out of wood. Without power, and not knowing how much longer it would take to turn it on, the next step was to walk into town to Aunt Gail's home. The walk was only around 2 miles up State Route 269, but it wasn't all that easy to walk with the wind and snow whipping in our faces and the temperatures still in the teens. We also could not see where the road was, and we just continued as best we could to follow the lines of trees, the mailboxes on the road that weren't buried, and the ruts in the road when we found any. We were bundled as best we could be, but we did not have snow suits or winter coats. I also did not have gloves. I had socks on my hands. Nearing the end of the walk, I pissed my pants. Once we got closer into town, we had to climb a huge snow pile and slide down the other side into the town's streets. Some of the streets were plowed with bulldozers and the snow was piled at the end of streets. When we slid over the hill of snow, it was like a war rescue. The National Guard was there to help us down and into warmth. We got a ride to our aunt's home a few blocks away. They had heat and food. My hands and fingers were so cold that they tingled like they fell asleep. But my hands and frozen snot on my mouth was the least of my concern.  The first order of business... change my pissy pants!  The insides of my pant legs were wet, and my legs were bright red.  As I said, we survived the Blizzard.   But there were many more storms headed our way.

# CHAPTER TWO

# The Downpour

As a pre-school aged child living in Ohio, I have minimal memories of living in our little box-shaped house. I remember the blizzard, our fluffy white dog, and the nice family that lived next door to us. Mom told us our little fluffy white dog, Buffy, ran away during the blizzard. And for many years that is what I came to believe. I assumed she just died in the storm. But later in my 40s, my mother told me poor Buffy froze to death in her doghouse during the blizzard. She said when we finally made it back home, they found her still frozen in her house. I don't know why the adults in our lives thought it was okay to leave the dog in that type of weather, but apparently, they had very little value for our family pet. This may be why I have a subconscious loathing for others who hurt animals or leave their pets in the cold. It is unconscionable!

A lot of childhood memories are created in the form of photographs. When you see a photo, you "remember" that day or that outfit. But sometimes, I think the photos create the memory, instead of the other way around. I guess it's true what they say these days, "Pics or it didn't happen." That is life in the literal sense to still frame that memory at that very moment in time. It helps to shape or create memories. Some of those moments in photos are of my Mexican mama and my Country-music playing dad in their bowling shirts. They were in a bowling league with the neighbors. The old Jolly Lanes bowling alley does not exist anymore at the other end of town. Another fun memory was of Lanny and Lola waiting outside for the school bus when a friend of our dad's showed up ready to fight. He came flying into the driveway honking his horn. Dad came running out buttoning up his shirt asking his buddy, Dick, "What's your fucking problem?" Dick rambled on about how bad Dad treated his wife, and that Dick was there to pick her up and take her away. Then the two of them squared up and started beating the hell out of each other. I was watching from the front step as they tossed each other around and threw punches at each other. Dad fell on his back and Dick was standing over him throwing punches while the jean jacket Dick was wearing started falling over his shoulders and getting in his way of seeing and punching. Lanny came over and started hitting Dick with his backpack telling him to get off his dad. Dad kept saying, "Son, I'm ok. I'm just resting. Have a good day at school buddy." Mom was looking from the window drinking her coffee. When the school bus came, Lanny and Lola ran onto the bus, Dick got back in his car and left, and I went inside to listen to Dad and Mom have a follow up fight about Dick showing up to take her away. We didn't know why someone would be coming to get her or why someone was going to take her away, but Dad was pissed as hell. And then he left the house to "finish some things with Dick."

We would have a babysitter come over so my parents could go to their bowling league. And also, when we had a babysitter over, Lola put both of her hands on top of the stove right after it had just been turned off. She burned both hands really bad and screamed in a lot of pain. The babysitter had to call the bowling alley to reach my parents so they could come home. Once they got there, Lola's hands had big blisters on the palms and almost every finger. They had to take her to the emergency room. She came home with bandages on both hands and had been crying the whole time. She had medicine for her skin and was eating a sucker that they told her she couldn't share because it was medicine for her; so, none of us tried to lick it.

One of my favorite pictures of myself is of me standing in the hallway with a saggy cloth diaper on. Do I remember that? Or did the picture trigger a story to go with it, not a real memory? In my mind, I do have two super vivid memories. But it is strange. The passing of time. And "memories." Are they real? Sometimes I feel like photos create or trigger "memories." Family stories that are told over and over are conditioned memories, and it makes it hard to remember what was real or what has been told so many times, that it just becomes another story we tell. Memories are weird to recount.

Two of my family stories involving me come to my mind in flashes. I can't say for sure if it is a story fed into my brain, or if I really do remember that far back. I remember two traumatizing events (hence the triggered memory) which led to me being taken to the hospital (not the piss-pants near frost bite during the blizzard). Both events occurred about age 4. I am not certain which one occurred first, so I will take a wild guess. I remember coloring at a table with my siblings. I will never know what possessed me other than sheer curiosity. I decided to stick a one-inch piece of a crayon up my nose. I will take a giant guess and say one of my older siblings, Lanny or Lola, had me do it, but I will never know for sure. My mother was advised of the Crayola being stuck up my nose hole. She, of course, panicked.  I remember her panic because she flung my ass around trying to shaken-baby the damn thing out. I know it is not uncommon for kids to pick their nose.  And I am aware that kids shove things up their nose, and they come out, fall out, or a parent can pluck it out. But for me, no such luck.  So lovingly I was held down by my face and arms and legs and hands so that my mother could shove fucking tweezers up my perfectly shaped nose to retrieve said crayon.  I will also point out that this traumatizing event and the second medical issue leading to a hospital visit, eventually became a large part of the reason I am profoundly claustrophobic.  After numerous digging expeditions, no such crayon was extracted from the nose hole.  This led to my dad being called.  He also had to take a turn at shaking and digging with no such luck.  I was taken to a small doctor's office in the next town over to the doctor who delivered me at the hospital.  The doctor seemed to be about 80 years old and had some age-related shakes.  This was also pretty fucking unsuccessful.  However, he had a super genius idea to put me in a pillowcase to keep me from wiggling around.  Ah, how advanced modern medicine has become since this episode.  The pillowcase did nothing except allow me to bite the old man, in which case he decided to knock me out.  After that, I am not sure how they got the crayon out.  But I'm certain each one of them probably shoved it so far up into my nose hole that it colored my fucking brain.  But it was out and that was the most important part.

The next childhood medical emergency occurred when our family was on vacation in Acapulco, Mexico with Aunt TiTi and Uncle William.  Again, this is one of those events that allows me to tell the story, but I am not certain if it is a memory of mine or a story I have heard from others so now I also "know" it happened.  Either way, we were poor, so I assume Aunt TiTi and Uncle William footed the bill. We were also grieving the loss of a child, and this was their way of helping our family get over what happened. We had family pictures on a pirate boat ride and a pirate posing for photos with the kids. I am in the photo but do not specifically remember being on the boat ride. What I do remember is riding in a car around mountains and sweating profusely in the back seat. I recall my siblings saying how thirsty they were and everyone's faces being red hot. One of the things I said to help our thirst, was to suggest we create as much spit in our mouths and swirl it around and swallow it. We tried that as much as we could on the mountainside drive and convinced ourselves we were really staving off thirst by drinking our own spit. We were gross.

We also had long days at the beach enjoying the sun and the water. We spent a lot of time on the lavish hotel room stairs running up and down and being yelled at by Aunt TiTi, mom, and the hotel staff. One of those Mexico nights, our family went out to eat at an all-you-can-eat buffet. My dad was bitching at me about being a picky eater. I was being asked to eat weird shit I wasn't used to, and I didn't want to eat it. I do love seafood, but I was trying to draw the line and didn't want to try things with tentacles. But I tried it. And I liked some of it, but the octopus was disgusting. My dad was sharing his food with me, and we pigged out. And then we both became ill. He was a big, chubby man so he could handle the dehydration from shitting and puking his brains out. But dainty little me, not so much. Puking and shitting, shitting and puking- the story of my life. By the next day, I was in a hospital in Mexico seeking medical care due to dehydration from food poisoning (probably the tentacles!) and not being able to keep anything down. I tried to tell them I was swallowing my own spit, but that didn't seem to help. The nurses felt the need to give me an IV and I felt the strong need to not cooperate. I can't remember how many times I was poked, or a nurse was kicked or bit, or how many of them ultimately sat on me to hold my psycho ass still until I was strapped to the bed frame. Then they held me still even further to put a freaking IV in the top of MY FOOT. A few of the other places didn't work, so this is what we resorted to. Once they finally got the IV in, I felt quite a bit better after a few hours. We were told over and over not to drink the water because that could make you sick. I remember being given bottled-water and thinking that was the weirdest thing ever. I thought drinking water in a bottle and drinking my own spit would keep me from being sick, yet here I was sick as a dog in the hospital. The nurses were really nice once they got me settled down and I wasn't acting like a feral cat. I got a cute stuffed animal, and they gave me some Mexican coins to remember my near-death ordeal by, and to commemorate more of the traumatic events that made me fearful of being in tight spaces and being held down.

We were pretty wild as a group. I am sure it was hard to keep track of all of us at once. We were all creative and found so many ways to occupy our time. We were seemingly unaware of the absence of our mother due to drinking and losing it over her dead son. We were unaware of the absence of our father playing in the bars, wandering and drinking and fighting. We didn't think anything of playing cowboys and Indians and getting the babysitter involved. We had her tied to a chair when our parents came home. I don't think that one ever came back to babysit a second time. Lanny would also ride his bike on State Route 269 with cars and semi-trucks beeping at him to get the hell out of the road. How we all survived to adulthood is a miracle. I thoroughly enjoyed the time my dad came home drunk, and my mom met him at the door with a shot gun. This happened more than once. They fought a lot. They broke a lot of things in the house. It seemed like we only ever had one parent functioning at a time. If one was home caring for us, the other was gone or drunk. Mom had some wild ways of reacting to him staying gone for days on end, and when he would come home, she was seething with anger. Often, he would be locked out of the house and had to break in. Sometimes when she would come home late from work, he would lock her out too. And oftentimes, they would throw each other's shit on the lawn. This type of behavior, people, is what we call TOXIC.

Mom worked at a truck-stop diner in Monroeville called Vanson's. She worked to help make ends meet. She always wore her hair long and her tan skin and high cheek bones really stood out. She worked off and on with a cook named Lee, who was just a few years out of high school. Lee was a hippie in the making with long, greasy hair, and he thought my mom, 10 years older than him, was just the most beautiful thing he had ever seen. He would often flirt with her which would drive his girlfriend, who also worked there as a waitress, crazy. Her name was Ellen, and she was foul-mouthed and rowdy. She lipped off to customers, co-workers, and her boyfriend, Lee, with whom she already had 2 young kids. She was a terrible waitress and was fired off and on. She would often chain smoke cigarettes with her kids in the car waiting for Lee to get off his shift and stop flirting with my mom. Sometimes she would leave the kids in the car with it running and go in the restaurant to make sure Lee wasn't talking to my mom. She was extremely jealous and with good reason.

We didn't stay in Bellevue much longer after Andrew died. That storm of '78 set the stage for what would become of my life. Chaos. Death. Moving. We had a cloud of turmoil that just seemed to follow us around. After that storm, I turned 5 and by summer, like nomads, my family decided to leave our little house and our little town and settle as far South as the parents could think to go. We moved to a beach town in Southern Texas. It was a predominately ethnically diverse city. We were mixed kids and should have fit in, but Lanny and I didn't get the Mexican memo. We were pale kids and stood out like sore thumbs. Lola and Christian fit right in due to their darker skin, hair, and eyes. Lanny and I were pale with freckles. Freckled Mexicans. LOL. I was the only "white" kid in my class. My dad had a few sisters living in the area also, Aunt Gail and Aunt Joy. They weren't far away, in a smaller area called Flour Bluff. Aunt TiTi and Uncle William loaned my parents the money to buy us a little home on Magnolia Street. We settled in a little gulf town called Corpus Christi. I loved our little street and neighborhood with our corner store, U-Totem. When we lived there so many years ago, it was the most beautiful place I have ever known. The trees on the street were magnificent Magnolias and the tallest trees I could ever imagine. I have many vivid memories of this place and wearing shorts in the winter months. One of the places we loved to go was an amusement park called Magic Isles. The sign had a Genie with a turban on it as their mascot. As little kids we loved to ride the motorcycles and cars that just went around in circles, and the best part was the bumper cars.

Our neighbors were an African American family with an older high school boy, a teen girl, and a younger girl my age that I liked to fight with. The high school boy was really tall, and he was a really good basketball player. We liked to follow Vincent around when he was dribbling the ball and try to get him to play with us. Our elderly neighbors to the other side had an orange tree in their backyard. They would take us to church for the first time in our lives and were the sweetest people. I remember one time Mrs. Young bought me a pair of dress shoes to wear to Sunday School. I suppose it was because she got tired of me trying to go barefoot all the time, and sometimes I did go to church with no shoes. I did have shoes, but I didn't want to wear them. They were hand me downs from Lola and I just wanted to go barefoot. Down the road, was another family that we became friends with as we had no local relatives in the area, therefore, no babysitters.

My dad would work for weeks out of town and my mom would work nights at Denny's restaurant down the 4-lane highway and over an overpass. We should not have been riding bikes on the overpass, but we did anyway. We were a little wild, and we would get bored or hungry at home and ride our bikes to the restaurant to see her and have her make us pancakes. I especially loved warm syrup and the fluffy scoop of butter on top!

Lola and I had bunk beds in our little room, and I enjoyed lifting my legs up and pushing on the slats of her upper bunk. She would get mad and yell at me, but I would keep doing it because it was funny. She would try to lean over the side and hit me and I would have to wiggle away from her. This was our usual routine at bedtime, and we were supposed to be quiet. On one of our nights goofing off, this noise made its way to our mother's ears. She came to the door and yelled at us to stop. When we continued to mess around, she came flying into the bedroom and gave us very little warning we were going to get our asses beat. She was enraged and started screaming at us for making noise. She pulled the curtain off the window and began pulling the curtain off the white, metal curtain rod. She pulled it apart and used half of it to start swinging at us. She had a hard time hitting me because the upper part of the bunk made it hard for her to swing into me. She did whack my feet and my hands when I was covering my head several times. She then turned to the top of the bunk and wailed away, striking Lola over and over with the curtain rod until it bent and was no longer useful. She cussed and spit and yelled in Spanish and was just out of control. Some of the whacks with the curtain rod grazed us with the end of it and cut our skin open with the sharp, metal ends. I had some cuts on the top and bottoms of my feet and Lola had some on her hands and thighs. Of course, we were quiet as church mice after this and cried ourselves to sleep. This was normal behavior to us, and normal nights when she was home consisted of her drinking and smoking cigarettes in the kitchen. We liked it better when she worked all night, and we didn't get hit with curtain rods or wooden spoons. We liked it better when she didn't grab our arms with her long fingernails and leave claw marks on the inside of our biceps. We also liked it better when we didn't have to go out to the yard and pick a switch for her to whip our backside. When she was really angry, we had to pull our pants down. We got a lot of spankings at night for being noisy. We got a lot of spankings for making messes and being rowdy in the house. Therefore, we liked to spend as much time outside as we could. I guess a hot-headed temper runs in our Mexican family. Mom would always cry and tell stories about being hit and slapped and beat by her mother and stepfather. But she did to us exactly what she always cried about being done to her. Thankfully, she didn't hit us with a hammer, but she did throw a screwdriver at Lanny one time and almost hit him right in the face.

Our nighttime routine was sporadic, and we never knew what to expect from one day to the next. For bath time, Lola and I would take as many bubbles in our bath as possible. I would use a cup and pour water over our heads. We were goofing around as usual and going as fast as we could. When I came up with the cup, Lola was going down for a scoop of water and I hit her right in the eyebrow with my cup and busted her head open. When blood came pouring out, we had to call for mom to come in. Of course, she was mad we were goofing off, and I brought an extra cup in the tub, when we were supposed to have one. I was slapped all over my wet, naked body and told to get out of the tub and get to my room. I grabbed a towel on my way out and ran to my room to dry off. Lola stood in the tub bleeding. Mom threw her a washcloth to cover her eye and stop the bleeding. A friend of mom's came over and put butterfly stitches on her gash.

Since we were alone most of the nights, and it seemed like it was all the time, we used to go to sleep in our school clothes so we wouldn't be late to school. We had a terrible concept of time, and didn't have alarm clocks or anyone guiding us to get ready in the morning. We were struggling to get to school on time. We got tired of being late. The plan was whoever got up first, was to wake everyone, and we would all get ready. One day we walked to school, and it was still dark out. I had no idea what time it was, so we all just played on the playground until the sun came up and other kids and teachers started arriving at school. On one occasion, we were walking in the pouring rain and accepted a ride from a stranger to school. Thankfully, there was a time in this world when people could trust each other, and there wasn't as much evil to be feared. I think about us getting in that car with some strange man today, and it makes me panic. Again, I have no clue how we survived our childhood!

The Texas sun was hot, and my hair was growing longer. I would try to brush it myself, but it was usually a mess. My mom never did my hair or helped us get ready. I had a huge knot on the underside of my hair by my neck that I couldn't brush out. I tried everything I could, but I couldn't get it out. So, I cut it off. Thankfully, I had long hair, and I could hide it from my mom. She never noticed. That isn't surprising as she really didn't notice much of anything we did unless we were getting in trouble. But one thing she had to notice was that my head was on fire with lice. Or as she would yell, piojos. I was sent home from school, and she had to help clean them out of my hair. We tried medicated shampoo and a comb. My mom was getting frustrated with my long hair trying to get the comb through the other knots in my hair. When she was washing my hair, she noticed the short hair on the underside and was enraged. She took a pair of scissors and cut the rest of my hair off. She said it was to even my hair out and to make sure she could get all the live lice and nits out of my hair. She cut my hair very short like a boy. It was short on top, with my ears cut out, and the back was a little longer. I had a girl mullet. And when I finally returned to school with short hair after being out for a few days, everyone knew it was due to lice. It was extremely embarrassing. Lola had lice constantly with me as well, and mom cut her hair off too. It was so hard to get rid of lice with long hair.

Since we were alone a lot and all night long, Child Protective Services paid us a visit. Someone reported a concern about us being left home alone. We lied and told the lady that Vincent, the high school boy next door was watching us and just went home for a bit to get some clothes and toys. At that point, the 4 of us ranged in age from 5 to 10. She called mom at work to come home, and she raced right to the house. She worked right down the road. We told her we just came home to get some things and she fake yelled at us and told us we needed to stay with the sitter. After that, we had to have a sitter or my mom's ass would be in trouble. Once dad found out about the CPS visit, he and mom got in a huge fight. He didn't understand why she was working so much and leaving us alone at night as he claimed he made plenty of money and she shouldn't have to. This led to his accusations that she is and has been continuously sleeping around with her customers. She was always flirty with her customers at her tables, and that is probably why Dick came to rescue her away from Dad back in Ohio. Dad was also having affairs and bar flings. They weren't very good marriage material for each other, and they were trying to raise a bunch of wild ass kids while they lived their own lives.

The family down the street became our saving grace since we didn't have family in the area. They would let us spend the night when mom worked. Their son and Lanny became friends, and they played on a pee wee football team together, the Cowboys. The teen sister, Maggie, would come over and babysit us, as well. Eventually, Maggie, Lola, and I all signed up to be cheerleaders for the football team. Dad helped coach, Lanny played, and Christian was the water boy. Dad loved sports; we all did. One night during one of the football games, the cheerleaders took the field for a cheer. I was one of the youngest on the team and I had to pee. Of course, right after the performance, I had to dead sprint to the potty. I didn't make it there in time and I pissed my pants. This seems to be another theme in my life. During these football games, I was introduced to Frito Pie: Fritos, chili beans, and cheese (and farts). My dad added onions, but I didn't care, I would eat it anyway. He would fart and blame them on anyone who smelled it. As he always said, "A rat smells his own hole first". Lanny was pretty good at football. He was also pretty good at baseball, and my dad also helped coach that team, as well. For as much as he was accused of being gone and a cheater, he sure did step in and stand in as a parent coach for Lanny's teams. The baseball team went to a city championship and won. I often wonder what ever happened to those boys on his team and what they grew up to be. To me, I felt these kids were going to grow up to be super stars. But who knows, maybe they did?

Dad somehow attached a huge, thick rope to one of the tall branches of our big tree in the back yard and we had a tire swing. We loved to push each other as high as we could. We also loved to twist the rope as tight as possible and spin out so fast we had to hold on tight. Sometimes we fell. But that never stopped us. We would try to go as fast as we could without falling off. We would all be filthy and scraped up and just loved the time we spent outside exploring. We also had a small garage behind us that my parents turned into an apartment and would rent out to random hippies and drifters. The house had a bar made of yellowed mirrors with squiggly designs on it. It reminded me of a huge disco ball.  When the house was empty, I would go in there and dance in my socks. Lola and I loved to dance and sing to our favorite records.  We would play the music so loud the neighbors would sometimes complain.

We also lived in a time when my mom could write us a note and send us to the convenience store at the end of the street and buy her a pack of cigarettes.  She smoked a lot.  She had the longest fingernails, and they were always painted red.  She cut her hair and was now wearing it in a puffy, curly afro, which was not a usual hairstyle for her.  On one occasion, we found her cigarettes, and decided to smoke them.  We lit the wrong ends and didn't know how to smoke until we practiced.  We all got sick.  We smoked several cigarettes, and I was probably only 7 or 8 years old.  Then we panicked when we decided she would notice cigarettes missing.  We buried the ones we smoked by the big tree with the tire swing and picked out the kid with the best handwriting, Lola, and wrote ourselves a note.  We scrounged up change and bought a new pack of cigarettes at the convenience store down the road, U-Totem.  Then we realized we needed to smoke some more because the old pack had at least a few missing.  I think I puked for 2 hours straight. Puking and pissing and shitting...my life's theme song.

Our lives continued to be one mess after another.  During the summers we spent most of our days outside playing and running up and down the streets. On the weekends dad would be home, and we would go to flea markets, out to eat, Magic Isle, and to the beach.  We had visits off and on from Aunt TiTi and Uncle William.  On one of their visits, Uncle William was a bit tipsy and sat a little too hard on our couch.  One of the legs broke and crushed under his weight.  He laughed so hard, and it was common for us to just laugh until our stomachs hurt when he was around.  Aunt TiTi and mom would bake pies and sweets, but dad would make the big meals in the kitchen. We would get new toys and clothes when they visited and that was the best part.

One summer when we were all home alone, Lanny damn near sliced the tip of his finger off with a tomato soup can. We had to get help from the renters in the garage house behind us to help stop the bleeding. And on another occasion, not knowing how to really cook bacon, little Christian put bacon in an already sizzling pan, and it popped up huge splats of grease right in his face. He had little blisters all over his face and eye lids. And although we thought we were safe from snowstorms; we were faced with another kind of storm headed our way just a few years later. The irony of it all. We ran away from cold weather and from the blizzard to the warmth of Texas only to find a hurricane bearing our own last name to come barreling up the Gulf Coast of Texas. Hurricane Allen hit in the summer of 1980. We boarded up our home the best we knew how. The renters decided to stay in the back house. Our family headed to Houston where some of my aunts were living and stayed for a few days as much of the coast was being urged to go inland to safety. When we got home, the house was perfectly fine, and one of the neighbor's cats was on our roof and it had new kittens. One of the best parts was that most of the streets were flooded. As usual, we felt this was a prime opportunity for us kids to put ourselves in danger and literally went swimming in the disgusting street flood waters, unsupervised, and having a good old time. I went under the water and came up right in the middle of a floating fire ant hill. I had ants and ant bites on my eyelids and ears, all over my face, shoulders, and neck. It seemed as though the storms would always follow us, or somehow, they would always find us. We didn't know any better. We were always moving. But no matter where we went, there would always be a storm.

# CHAPTER THREE

# The Storm

Mother was strict and would slap the shit out of you if you looked at her cross-eyed. I don't know if that was because she had a short temper, or we were just a bit too much to handle. It probably didn't help that she had epic mood swings and was drinking big clear bottles of liquor that would get you sad. I didn't know what it was, but I knew she was drunk and sad. We spent time playing arcade games at the laundromat behind our house. I was so good at Mrs. Pac-Man. I held the high score at one point until TAZ beat my high score. Fuck you very much TAZ whoever you are for crushing my high score I only held for one fucking day! It became more and more noticeable that not only were we alone a lot, but so was mom. My dad was gone a lot more than usual. When he finally came home, he had big wads of money, and we would go out to eat. Usually, he knew the best places. Monterrey House was our favorite. They had creamy caramel candies in wax paper wrappers in the tortilla chips they would place on your table. These were the best sweets you can sink your teeth into.

Like pure sugar! My dad had a sweet tooth. And so did I. On a lot of our trips, it seemed like usually mom didn't want to go, or sometimes she wasn't invited.

On one occasion dad came home, and my mom was sick. He questioned her for what seemed like hours about being sick, how she got sick, what she was sick from, and why no one else in the house had what she had. To us, she seemed the same. She was tanked from working all night and drinking all day and probably was hung over. But he accused her of being pregnant and a huge fight ensued. She said he always wanted her to get pregnant and have more kids but as we remember it, he didn't want her getting pregnant and was telling her we didn't need any more kids to take care of. He checked her birth control and found that they were all empty little bubbles where a pill should be in the pill pack. She acted surprised that all her pills were gone and started blaming the kids for getting into her purse. She pointed the finger at me and said she finds me in her purse all the time and I use her lip stick. I never used her lip stick. I couldn't stand the way it made her look like a clown, and I never tried to put her makeup on. But she threw me right under the bus and told my dad that I must have eaten her birth control pills.

She grabbed me by my hair and pulled me into the bathroom and forced my head over the toilet while she stuck her finger in my throat. She was scratching and stabbing the back of my throat with her long fingernail trying to force me to puke. She was screaming at me to tell the truth, to tell everyone that I ate her pills thinking they were candy. I was gagging and crying and snotting all over myself. Eventually I puked but it was nothing but yellow stomach acid and blood from my throat. It burned coming out of my nose. I hadn't had anything to eat that day and was so glad to see dad walk in the door, as I knew we were going to get a chance to go eat. He stood in the bathroom doorway watching her try to prove that I ate her pills.  He eventually pulled her away and told her to leave me alone.  One of the things he said to her is that she can't just have another kid to replace the one that died, and reminded her that she was doing a shitty job already taking care of the ones she has. When she stood up, leaving me sobbing draped over the toilet, he slapped her across her face so hard.  I squeezed my eyes shut and curled up in a ball on the bathroom floor.  Before she walked out of the bathroom, she told him he better whoop my ass.  She went into their bedroom and slammed the door.  After the fighting and the yelling and the crying, he took me into the bedroom and told me to sit on the bed.  He hit the bed a few times, making a noise like he was spanking me.  He said he didn't know who to believe, but he told me that if I did eat her pills, I was going to grow boobs as big as Dolly Parton.  And I felt crazy thinking that maybe I did eat her pills, and mom was right that I didn't remember doing it.  I was only 8, and I didn't know if maybe it was possible I did forget.  I secretly started hoping I would grow boobs as big as Dolly.  Then we left the house without her. And I was glad.  My dad took us to Houston to Astro World and we were gone for several days.

When we came home after our Astro World trip, things started to get really ugly around the house.  My mom's car was returned to the bank and our electricity was turned off.  We ran an extension cord to the neighbor's home to keep our refrigerator on.  My dad came home less and less, and things just weren't right.  One day, there was arguing in the house, and we were outside playing on the tire swing.  We ran in the house and stood in the kitchen trying to hear what was going on and decide what we should do. Lanny went in the living room to see what was happening and started screaming at my dad.  The living room was in complete disarray.  My dad was standing over top of my mom choking her, yelling at her, cussing.  We don't know what she did this time or what the fight was about, but Lanny ran and got his baseball bat. He squared up and started to hit dad with it on his back and the back of his head. He was stunned and stumbled on the floor and fell off mom as she finally sat up cussing in Spanish and spitting her words at him. Dad went out the front door and mom told us all to go to bed. It was still daylight out.

One night, not long after the living room fight, we were awakened by commotion again in the living room. We all 4 woke up and collected in the hall that led out to the kitchen. Around the corner was the living room. While we were standing quietly, trying to listen to what was going on, we heard a low growling sound coming from the living room. This was a sound none of us had ever heard before, but it sounded like an animal. We stood in silence listening again and heard thrashing and glass breaking and the growl. We decided to send a scout around the corner to look and see what was going on in the living room. So, of course we convinced the dumb little one the easiest. Christian was just about 6 at the time and rounded the corner with an exaggerated tip-toeing motion, and his hands held out in front of him like a bunny. He tip-toed louder than we had hoped out to the kitchen to see into the living room. However, when he tip-toed back and his eyes were wide, and he appeared scared. He said, "There's a wolf in the living room!" in a voice that should have been a whisper, but it was not. So, since no one could believe what he was saying, I was sent to do a follow up peek for the group. I did not tiptoe. I stomped because I was annoyed, and I was tired, and I wanted to go back to bed. And now I was scared because there was a wolf in the living room. I peeked around the corner into the living room and noticed first that the house was in shambles. Pictures that were on the walls were broken on the floor. There was glass everywhere. The coffee table was turned upside down, and the couch was tipped over. The front door to the house was standing wide open and the porch light was on. There was also a lamp on the ground, and the light bulb broken all over the floor. There was just enough light coming through the front window and from the door to see there was in fact a wolf in the living room. My heart was beating fast. My eyes were sleepy, and I rubbed them hard to see again what I was seeing. When I looked again, I saw what looked like 4 legs and a lot of wet, black hair. And the growling was retching and gurgling, the most god-awful sound. Then the head turned to face me. I was frozen in fear as I noticed the arm raise up and point to me, or at me, or behind me. I couldn't tell. But what I did notice was the hand had a long, red fingernail. And the wolf was my mom on all fours gurgling blood out of her nose and mouth and gasping for breath. She was ordering me back to my room with that fingernail.

So, I turned and walked back to the bedroom we all shared and hit my little brother upside the head, calling him stupid. Everyone asked me what was going on, and I told them it was mom making the noises and that she told me to go back to bed, so that's what I did. I wasn't frightened. I wasn't sad. I barely cared that my mother's face was so bloody it seemed black. I thought maybe she was getting spanked and in trouble for hurting me and making me puke, when I didn't do anything wrong. I felt like that might be why she was getting in trouble. The way of the world to me was so literal, if you do something wrong, you should be punished. I was still angry with her for being punished when I didn't do anything wrong. Secretly, I felt that she deserved it. I felt bad because I was supposed to feel bad for her. Her hair was wet from sweat and blood. She was disfigured as her lips and her nose were swollen and puffy. She was gasping and gagging, having been beaten to a literal bloody pulp. She was re-filling her lungs with air, as she almost had the life choked out of her. Her throat was raw and sore wrapped with red markings from the hands that squeezed her neck.

It wasn't the first time we saw a bloody face, bloody nose, broken household items, broken pictures, broken windows, and black eyes. I was desensitized to it as this was seemingly normal and a routine part of our day or night. I thought of it as punishment in the way we were punished. I didn't understand what was happening to her was wrong. We didn't know life was to be any other way. This was all we knew. The living room was always a mess. My mom had a pretty large pair of sunglasses, and she wore them often. In our world, we usually saw the after-effects. On a rare occasion, we saw the actual fighting happening in front of us.

The fact that our parents divorced was no surprise. My mother needed to leave my dad to prevent further abuse. Dad was often accusing my mom of cheating on him. The fighting was out of control, but I never saw a cop at our house any time. No one called the cops, not my mom, not the kids, no one. While we knew nothing of the word divorce, we knew absence, separation, and loss. We didn't get any explanation. No one told us what was changing or why. It just started to change. Our days changed. Our mom changed. We just woke up the next day to the next change which was our normal.

When my dad left and moved out, my brother Lanny went with him. My mom picked up the house and the pieces of her life and tried to do things on her own without any support from dad. We didn't see my dad or Lanny for a long time, almost a year. I think it was around Easter when dad left with Lanny. Mom was still working at Denny's. At school we were doing a project and the teacher was asking for eggshells, only cracked open with a small hole at the top. I was so happy to bring in eggshells just like she asked from my mom's work, enough for the whole classroom the next day. She even let me help in the cafeteria to wash them out so other classes could use some.

Mom also found a new boyfriend. I think mom may have met "Rick" at Denny's, but no one ever really asked her. He seemed nice most of the time. Mom seemed better, happy. She still was drinking and smoking, but she wasn't lonely anymore. Rick was around more and more, and he liked to play a game that terrified me. He would take a blanket and throw it over me, trap me inside and hold me down under it. He thought it was funny, but I would literally hyperventilate and scream and cry as I was extremely claustrophobic. I would punch and kick and just go ape shit under the blanket until he let me out. He would just laugh and then do the same thing to Christian who would have the same reaction as well. Rick seemed to think it was fun and he would just walk away like nothing happened leaving us in puddles of tears and sweat and terror. The feeling of being trapped was awful. The next feeling was being smothered and unable to breathe. And then it was just sheer panic. No amount of screaming or kicking would make him quit. He stopped when he wanted to. Christian and I would try to run, and sometimes he would just throw a blanket over us while we were running and trap us wherever we fell. And then he was on top of us, smothering us. When he was smothering Christian, I would hide. And when he was smothering me, Christian would hide. He only ever did this when he was watching us while mom was working. And he didn't try this with Lola as she was bigger and better able to protect herself.

Rick was a really tall man standing at 6'4", and he overpowered Christian and I with ease. It became so routine, that Christian and I would cry or start faking sick when mom would start getting ready for work. She would ask us in front of Rick why we didn't want her to leave, and we were never able to tell her that we felt that one of these days we would be smothered to death.  We became deathly afraid of Rick and would hide in our rooms and stay out of his way as best we could while mom was working.

By Christmas, Rick was around even more and seemed to be at the house every day.  And he bought us all new bikes. Except for Lanny. He wasn't there. Christian was a daredevil and liked to ride his bike trying to pop wheelies.  Our first day riding, he flipped himself over the handlebars and smashed his face on the curb.  That was probably the first of many sets of stitches for that kid! Lola didn't have her bike long, as it was stolen off our porch.  She started riding my bike and I would just run alongside her waiting for my turn on my own bike.  It was pink and gray, and I thought it was the best present I had ever had, even better than Aunt TiTi and Uncle Wally's gifts. We also got a giant stocking stuffed with toys.  It was hanging on the wall at Denny's that you could win by putting your name in a drawing.  When mom won it for us, it had so many toys in it.  We couldn't hardly believe it. Life seemed to quiet down, and we were getting into a new routine. A new normal.  But something new was always next.

I sat on the porch waiting for the little boy down the street to come over.  Ernesto said he would be there, and I waited and waited.  We were going to play in the yard.  We had a duck named Linda.  And we had a few chickens I wanted to show him.  We could also pick some oranges from the neighbor's tree if none had fallen off in our yard by then. We would have to check.  But first, he would need to get here. I kept looking to my left down the street direction where we headed for school or for U-Totem.  But to my surprise, he came walking up the sidewalk from the other direction.  Confused, I asked him why he was coming from that way.  Ernesto said a few houses down, across the street, their dog was out, and he was afraid to walk any closer because it was "going crazy" and it bit him before. So, he had to turn around and go around the block. I hopped up and accepted the challenge to see exactly what was going on. We walked down the street on my side of the road, and sure enough, the dog was on the porch. But it hadn't seen us yet.

Ernesto said, "April, I dare you to walk across the street and walk past that house." I laughed because I couldn't believe he was so scared of this dog. It was so small. It was a little, white chihuahua. I told Ernesto I would be happy to do it. I crossed the street and Ernesto hid behind a bush. I walked fast and as soon as I got to the sidewalk leading up to the house, the dog saw me. And just like Ernesto said, he started to bark and growl. I kept moving, looking across the street at Ernesto, and he started to point to the porch behind me. When I turned around, I realized the dog was running down the walkway. At first, I thought it was on a chain, so I didn't change my pace. However, once the little, white chihuahua turned onto the sidewalk behind me, I took off running. The dog nipped my heels and jumped up and bit me on my ass! The homeowner came out of the front door and yelled for the little demon dog from hell to get home. I just kept running all the way down to the end of the street. Ernesto came running too. I looked back and noticed my sock had a little rip and a little blood on it. My shorts were ripped at the bottom from the snaggle tooth. And my butt was burning from the bite.

By that time, we were closer to Ernesto's house than mine, so he decided he was just going to go back home. Ernesto said the dog bit the back of his leg, so he never goes by there when he is out. I told him I had to go home and tell my mom what happened. When I came in the door, the neighbor man in a red shirt was already sitting in the kitchen talking to my mom. She said, "Sit the fuck down, April." I sat on the chair and my little ass cheek stung and burned a little. She asked if Ernesto and I were teasing the dog. I told her no, that I was just walking past the house and the dog chased me. She slapped me across the face and called me a "little fucking lying bitch." And she spit her words and enunciated way too long. I could tell she was drunk. She smelled like it. She sent me to my room, and I could hear her telling the neighbor that she would "take care of it." After the neighbor left, the door to my room flew open and she started yelling. She said she was embarrassed to have such disrespectful kids running all over the streets acting like idiots. She wanted me to apologize to the neighbor. When I stood up to walk out the door, she kicked me right on my butt where the dog bit me. My hips flew forward, and my head snapped back, then I fell on my knees. She said, "Change your clothes first. You're filthy."

I changed my shorts and walked across the street and down to where the little demon dog lived. I walked up to the door and the little dog was barking his fool head off at the knocks on the door. When the man in the red shirt came to the door, he said "Quiet down, Tito." And he did. The little demon quit barking, sat down, and started quivering. He asked if I would like to come inside, and I said, "No, thank you." I told him, "My mother wanted me to come and say sorry to you and Tito. So. I am sorry." He told me not to come past his house anymore and get Tito fired up and that he told my mother I let Tito off his chain. Which was a lie. He said Tito has never bit anyone before. Which was another lie. I said, "Ok. Well, have a good day." And when I turned around, I mumbled under my breath, "little fucking lying bitch." He said, "I'm sorry, what did you say?" I turned back around and said, "Have a good day." I couldn't wait to tell Ernesto how this whole fiasco turned out when we went to school on Monday.

Then as luck would have it, I had to miss school for a while. All of us kids ended up with the chicken pox at the same time. We got to do schoolwork at home and mom would take care of us. We were lathered up with pink lotion and whatever other home remedies she could think of. She was always mixing up weird pastes and oils and home-made salves to put on our sores to help dry them up. One terrible one was a paste made with peppers and it burned. We had an Aloe plant and she used that a lot to put on everything. She wrapped up our hands with socks so we would stop itching and busting our spots open. Lola had some spots on her face and neck. We did the best to let them dry out and heal so we could go back to school. But I didn't mind doing work at home.

It seemed like it took weeks for us to get better. Rick wasn't around when we were sick with chicken pox, so we didn't get him sick. Mom was sad and crying a lot. She was sick all the time and throwing up every day. She would play sad songs and drink in the kitchen. Her music would be up so loud it kept us up at night. One of my favorite songs I loved to hear her playing was *Sailing* by Christopher Cross. Listening to the song all the time, I think she was thinking about Andrew and missing Lanny. That's who I would think of when I heard the song. And my dad. I missed him a lot, but I don't think mom missed him at all. I missed him cooking meals and taking us places. With mom, she went to work and home, and we didn't go anywhere or do anything. We also had to learn to cook better meals because she wasn't much of a cook. Dad made big meals. Now we had burritos from any leftovers. If we had chicken, she would pick the remaining chicken off any bones and put it in a tortilla with anything else left over for the day. Sometimes it was chicken and salsa, sometimes it was chicken and eggs and cheese. They would be folded up, wrapped in plastic wrap, and put in the freezer to thaw out and eat later. Sometimes, we would warm them up in the oven. When you bit into it, you never knew what you are going to get. My favorite was eggs, bacon, and cheese. Burrito surprise. That is what we called it.

One night, we overheard her talking to one of the neighbors in the kitchen. She was drinking, smoking, crying, and playing loud music. She was talking about Rick, and that he was mad at her. She told the neighbor she was pregnant. We all just looked at each other and were freaking out that she was going to be having another baby in our house. Christian thought it would be fun to have a baby in the house so he could have someone that would play with him. We were all just feeling weird as we have never really been around a baby before. But Lola and I knew Dad would be mad. He always said we didn't need another baby. We didn't quite understand that it wasn't his baby.

Eventually we got to go back to school from the chicken pox outbreak and were actually glad to be able to eat school lunches again. Burrito surprise was getting old. But a few short days later, I got sent home again after a visit to the school nurse. I was feeling sick and sore, and my ribs hurt really bad. The nurse took my temperature, and I had a fever. She said I would have to go home. When she lifted my shirt, she found more chicken pox on one side of my back along my rib cage. This second round of pox, the school nurse called shingles. I had pain in my side, and it hurt so bad to even breathe. It felt like I was whipped with a switch. It burned like the bite from Tito. No one knew why I got this second round as it was so odd. I would lay around with salves from the aloe plants, and peppers, and whatever else mom could make into something to spread on my skin. She told Lola and Christian not to touch me, so I didn't give them my disease. And I was stuck at home with burrito surprise, and now I didn't have anyone to talk to. The blisters and sores seemed to heal after a few weeks again, and I was allowed to go back to school. However, when I got back to school, no one wanted to play with me at recess, so they didn't get my skin disease from me. But I didn't care, I wasn't at school for the friends anyway. Ernesto and his sister, Janie, were really the only ones who ever spoke to me. Janie was pale like me, except she could speak Spanish. I couldn't. She had long, red hair. She always wore pig tail braids. They lived right down the road, and I would see them all the time on the weekends riding bikes or roller skates down the street.

While Lanny and Dad were gone, Dad found a new place for them to stay while he made a plan to get his kids away from mom. He also found a new girlfriend. He ended up at a few of the aunts' places and borrowed money from Grandma Rose for a lawyer. But before he got his ducks in a row, Dad ended up in a psychiatric hospital due to depression. He threatened to kill himself while in a drunken stupor. Lanny was 12 at that time, and dad told him if he didn't go with him, he would kill himself. Lanny felt responsible for keeping him alive and ensuring nothing happened to him. He stayed with dad for this reason and to be his protector, like the time he was hitting Dick on the back with his backpack to protect his dad. Lanny was going to watch out for Dad the best he knew how.

The time frames of my life are hard to keep track. I try to keep things in order by holidays. Some were good. Some were fucking horrible. And then, suddenly, my dad was back. He met us at school one day while we were waiting for mom to pick us up. Dad was acting weird but we were excited to see Lanny. Dad said he would have to hide so mom didn't see him, or she might just drive off. He walked us around the corner where the fence hid the school dumpsters to wait for mom and he could be out of sight. She pulled up to the sidewalk and I could see her while peeking around the corner. So, I waved to everyone to come on and get in the car. I grabbed the door handle and just stepped inside with one leg, and everyone came around the corner at the same time to load up into the car, including dad. As soon as mom saw him, she stepped on the gas and took off while I was hanging onto the door and had one leg in the car. I hopped on one leg outside of the car as fast as I could while I hung on, and Lanny and Lola screamed for help. She was going too fast, and I had to let go and fell between the road and the sidewalk right when she turned onto the road. Thankfully she turned, or she would have run me over. I was petrified and scraped up on the side of my face and my knuckles. My backpack protected me the most once I rolled and skidded with it still on my back.

Dad walked home with us and waited for a while, but once it got dark, he said he had to get going. He said he would be back the next day. And he did come back and was around a few days in a row to talk to mom which usually turned into fighting. He would take us all out to eat and for short visits. He would comment about the house being messy and the kids being hungry. We went to the best places to eat and lots of visits to the beach. We loved to jump with the waves, and dad would drive his truck right up to the water where we would have pop and candy and snacks for the whole day. Up and down the beach, there were little blue bubbles of dried-up jelly fish we loved to pop with sticks. Eventually karma came to get me as I found myself surrounded by them in the water and couldn't swim away from the group without being stung on my leg. Dad took me to the lifeguard shack, and they poured something cold on my leg that made it feel better but only for a few seconds. The lifeguard told my dad to just keep an eye on my breathing and that the discomfort would eventually go away. And I wasn't allowed back in the water. I sat on the tailgate of Dad's truck watching the waves crash and hoping no one else got stung. I saw one more little girl head to the shack grabbing onto her arm; she was probably stung also. Even getting stung, a beach day was always better than home. I loved the crunchy saltwater hair, the sunshine on my face, and not thinking about anything except fun.

After one of the visits with dad, we didn't go back home. And no one explained to us what was happening around this time. Evidently there was a court hearing, and dad had an attorney. Mom was uneducated and didn't speak English well. They were only recently divorced, and she was already pregnant by another man. She wasn't taking good care of us kids. We were dirty, hungry, and unsupervised more than ever. It was shocking for that point in time, but full custody was awarded to dad. The key to him obtaining custody was the wishes of my brother to stay with dad and not go back to live with mom. He was about 12 now and basically spoke for us all. The court felt if he wanted to live with my father, we should all remain together. No one knew Lanny was told by my father that if he didn't get custody of all 4 of us, he would kill himself. My dad also reported some inappropriateness on the part of the hippies and drifters who lived in the back house coming in and out of our house as they pleased. This was true, as they never visited or came in much until dad was gone. Then they were spending a lot of time in the house with us kids and with mom. There were also allegations about one of them going pee in our bathroom while Lola was in the shower as they didn't have water in the back house for some reason. None of us thought anything of it, but evidently the court did. Dad always accused mom of sleeping with the men in the house behind us. He always found someone he thought she was cheating with, probably because he had several girlfriends on the side.

When we left with dad, mom was pregnant. Dad knew. The court knew. And to them and everyone else, it seemed like she didn't want us. She didn't put up any fight for us. She didn't ask Uncle William or Aunt TiTi for help or for money for an attorney. They were more than capable of helping her. But she never asked. She didn't ask for visitation. She was never affectionate. She didn't seem to know how to be our mother and didn't seem like she wanted to be our mom anymore. Everything we said or did was a big inconvenience to her. She hated having to feed us every day. She didn't want to have to look after us and left us alone a lot so she could go work. She tried to act like a good mom around Rick, but when he was gone, she went back to ignoring us. She was extremely wrapped up in her new boyfriend, and in our eyes, we didn't feel important. Well, we never felt important, so we felt even less important. It didn't help that she was drinking all the time, either. Yes, even when she was pregnant. And smoking. Everything she detested about other people, she did and was doing. When we went with dad, it seemed like the parent who wanted us the most, is the parent who ended up with us. Mom was never ordered to pay a penny of child support to this man who would now be raising 4 children on his own. And she was perfectly fine with that as she had a new baby on the way that would be a start to her new life. And just like that, she lost every single one of her children. Well, I think it is more appropriate to say she lost one and gave up on the other 4. How traumatizing?

We were replaced in our mom's life with the new baby on the way and dropped like we were nothing. It seemed like that is all she ever wanted, a replacement baby. And now that she was getting one, we were no longer wanted or needed. Dad was a terrible husband and a terrible man to the women in his life. It seemed life was giving him a chance to redeem himself as a father. And in the end, he also got what he wanted, and we were at his mercy.

When we moved, everything was so sudden, so unplanned. I never got to say goodbye to any of my teachers or to even let Ernesto and Janie know that I wasn't coming back the next year. I had just finished 2$^{nd}$ grade. I was crushed that I was leaving the only school I had ever known. Oak Park Elementary school was the only safe place I knew. My teachers were kind. I was fed regularly. I was excited about learning. I received an honorary Library card in kindergarten because I was one of the few kids who could read when I entered school. I was asked to come down to the principal's office that year, and I was so nervous because I thought I was in trouble. Turns out, my Kindergarten teacher, Mrs. Bridges, advocated for me to get a library card. The meeting with the principal was so I could read to her. After that, I could get the library card. I was so proud and excited. I took home as many books as I was allowed every week. Sometimes I did my schoolwork as fast as I could so I could read my books. And they weren't just words. It was information and a way to fill my head with as many words and stories as I could. I always asked mom to ask for extra work in my progress notes to school. I just wanted to have more to do at home.

I loved napping on mats in school in kindergarten. At the start of the year, we had to bring a photo of ourselves. I sat in our small living room, with my hair in pig tails and smiled for the camera while my dad took my picture on the polaroid camera. It came out and I waved it around until the full picture showed up. I put it in my folder of papers to take with me to school on the first day. I walked to school with Lola and Lanny. We learned colors and shapes and we had a school performance on the stage in the cafeteria where I loved to eat. When the red curtains went up, we had a song and would march around holding our shapes or our color when it was sung in the song. I had a red circle on a stick.

My 2$^{nd}$ grade teacher, Ms. Castaneda, was the most beautiful lady I had ever seen in my life. She always wore red lipstick and had beautiful, long black hair. I was encouraged in the school environment, and I found refuge in the classroom setting. I felt smart at school. I craved the encouragement. I needed a classroom. I hoped wherever we went had a good school.   I was sadder about leaving school than I was leaving my mom. I was sad about leaving the tire swing behind.  She got pregnant on purpose. She didn't really care about Rick either. She just wanted the baby.  And then, we left our mom.  We left our school. We left our friends.  We left our little house on Magnolia Street with just the clothes on our backs, wondering what could possibly be next.

# CHAPTER FOUR

# The Wind

We drove and drove and stopped to sleep on one occasion in some random town. We stopped at a gas station and dad went in to get some snacks and make a phone call. I could tell it was mom on the phone, and he was talking really softly so I could only hear a few words here and there. But I could hear her yelling on the phone at him and I could distinctly hear her saying, "Hit me with your best shot motherfucker." Her English wasn't very broken with that statement, and it was clear as day she was pissed about something. When he was done with the call at the pay phone, we sat on the bench next to him and he was writing things down in a notebook. He sat there writing for a while and eventually someone else came to use the phone. Us kids were getting bored, so we were going back and forth to the truck waiting for him to get in and go. At one point I ran back to where he was sitting on the bench and started whining about what was taking so long. He gave me the dirtiest look while he was writing, and I interrupted him. He was listening to the man on the phone share his credit card information over the phone and dad was trying to write down the numbers and other information. But I made so much noise when I ran up, that he missed a few numbers. Dad was pissed at me, and I ran back to the truck to hide. I had no idea what a credit card was, but apparently, I ruined his plan for whatever he was going to do, so I guess we will never know.

We continued driving and ended up outside of New Orleans. We didn't know anyone, and we weren't allowed to go anywhere. We didn't have any toys but the family next door to us, the Freedman family, had a trampoline. We spent hours jumping on it as it was something so new to us. We couldn't get enough of it. Our place was a condemned home. And Mr. Freedman offered my dad a job. Mr. Freedman had an accent like one I have never heard of before. When he found us jumping on the trampoline at all hours of the day and night, he said, "Oooooweeeee Lahneee. You skerred mah." It always took a minute to understand him with such a huge southern drawl. But it was cute. He was a big man and wore jean overalls. We stayed in one room in the home due to holes in the floor and rodents. My dad was clearly in some kind of depression, but we didn't know much about why or what was really going on with him. All we saw was that he would drink himself to sleep. He slept most of the time when he wasn't working. We were hungry most of the time. We didn't have much food at home. We spent a lot of the summer on job sites with dad. Lanny would help him with the dry wall, and Lola and I would wash out buckets, drywall knives and brushes. Christian would usually just play around and break stuff. He always seemed to be in the way. We loved to sweep up the floors and keep things clean. Eventually, when dad needed a new bucket of mud, we learned how to use the mixer to blend the powder and water into the texture he needed. He and Lanny made a good team. It was fun watching dad walking around with stilts on. It was also fun when the job was done, and it was payday! We were so glad for school to start for the breakfast and lunch and less work for us. We didn't have much and certainly couldn't afford a nicer place. We didn't know anything more about life other than we were with him, and we didn't live with our mom anymore. I didn't know why; it was just the way it was.

My brother enrolled in a new school named after a President, and I can't remember the name of my school. We rode a bus for the first time, and it was scary. I was always so nervous that I would get off at the wrong school or get off the bus at the wrong house. Thankfully, I had Lola who always seemed to know exactly where to get off. But now, we also had to make sure Christian was paying attention with us. I met new kids in my class and had another new teacher. We were the "new kids", and everyone was interested in finding out "where we came from." When we had a writing assignment about who lived in our home, my teacher pulled me to the side to ask me why I didn't have a mom on my paper. I tried to think of how to explain it and was stuttering over the words. She said, "It's ok, April. We can talk about that another time." And by another time, she meant, with another person. Someone from the office came to get me out of class and take me to the school counselor. She was asking about my writing assignment and not having a mom in the house. I did the best I could to explain that my dad just got us from my mom. She asked a lot of questions about her and what she was like. I told her that she just didn't live with us and that she speaks Spanish. The school counselor said, "Oh I see. She had to go back to live in Mexico?" I said I actually didn't know where she was living, and that was that. I told her we haven't seen her in months. She told me she was sorry my mom left us and was just thrilled that dad was raising such a smart little girl. I still buried myself in schoolwork and reading. I loved to write words and spell. I asked for as much work as I could get. I needed something at home to pass the time.

On occasion, I would get to my desk, and I would have a little something new. One day it was two new rainbow-colored pencils. One day, it was a small notebook for journal writing. One day, it was a little package of hair ponies and a brush in a little pouch. I especially loved this as I didn't have a brush at home. Mrs. Smith gave us writing assignments once a week. She would give us a question on the board at the beginning of the week, and every Friday, we had to turn it in. I loved to do these assignments. I would write all week long, and I always turned in the longest answers. One of the kids in the class called me a "suck-up." I thought that meant I was smart because I always got 100% on these assignments. The last question before Christmas break was, "What do you want for Christmas?" Of course, my writing assignment was going to be longer than everyone else's. I can't just put down a gift I want.

*"If I could have what I want for Christmas, it would be to have happiness. I would want all the kids to be happy and smile. For Christmas, I would just ask to have money. We would have dad go to the store and buy us some food to make a big pot of chili. I would want dad to play loud music while he is cooking and be happy, laughing and dancing like we used to in Texas. I would want him to show us all the secret ingredients he adds to it that make it so good. He always keeps his recipes a secret. I would want to know the secret recipes. I would want crackers and onions and cheese to go on top. The best part is a piece of white bread with butter to dip in the chili. It would be the best day if he would just wake up and be happy and get his guitar out and play music and sing songs. I love it when he sings us funny songs and makes us laugh. The best Christmas would be if we could all be together at the table laughing and telling jokes, even mom, if she still loves us. If I could have my brother Andrew*

*back just for one day that would be the best Christmas ever. I don't want a gift; I just want happiness."*

After our last assignment was turned in, I ended up in the counselor's office again with Mrs. Smith. Mrs. Smith had tears in her eyes and asked me if I had a wish list for Christmas. She explained the writing assignment as something I would want, like a gift. I told Mrs. Smith I never made a Christmas list before. I told her I would be ok with something like extra schoolwork or papers I can take home or a book. At this point, both the counselor and my teacher were crying. I had no idea what their problem was. I guess I didn't understand the assignment. And I started to feel tears welling up in my eyes, as well. I told her I could do the writing assignment over, and I didn't want to have a bad grade. I could think of other things to add to the list I would want. I didn't know she meant toys. I told her I really didn't want any toys. I breathed in and out really slow, so they didn't know I was about to cry. I pinched myself as hard as I could on my leg to distract myself from feeling like crying. Mrs. Smith said the writing assignment was graded already and it was a 100%. She just wanted to ask me if I had anything at home that I liked to do for fun. She asked about games, and dolls, and toys. I told her no. The only thing we had was a deck of cards and we knew how to play war. I told her the neighbors had a trampoline, and we played on that a lot. She seemed to be interested in knowing what kinds of things we liked to do to pass the time. I told her just being outside and playing was really fun for us. Mrs. Smith was very sweet, and she always called me a shining star. Once she got all her questions answered, she had to stop in the office before they headed back to the classroom. She reassured me that I got a good grade and told me not to worry! But I did worry. I worried the whole time that I would not get a 100% on this paper because I didn't know what toys to write.

With Christmas rolling around soon, I was dreading the break from school. At this school, we got there early on the bus and had breakfast and then we got lunch too. We didn't have much at home so we really depended on the days we could eat at school. We didn't even have a Christmas tree. Once we were on break from school, we were struggling to find things to do to fill our day since dad wasn't on a job at that time. Jobs seemed to slow down, and we didn't have much money. We got boxes of food from a food pantry. We tried a cookie recipe and cooked in the oven, and they were good. They were hard. But they tasted good. We liked to fry biscuits in a pan and sprinkle them with cinnamon and sugar. We got really good at following box directions. Dad didn't follow any directions. He always seemed to just throw everything together and it just turned out awesome. He would always praise our cooking when we made dinner. He just didn't seem to want to cook lately.

By Christmas Eve, we didn't have electric. So, we were eating cereal from the box without any milk, crackers and soup in the can, and no more cooking. We never really made a big deal out of Christmas, because it just was never much of a big deal around our house. The worst thing of all about Christmas: it was mom's birthday. And we wondered if she was celebrating without us because we never felt like celebrating her, that's for sure. We didn't even know how old she was.

On mom's birthday, we awoke to someone knocking on the front door. It was really early for us to get up, but Lanny jumped up to open the door. We thought at first it might be mom. We found an extra-large black, plastic garbage bag on the front porch. We were all astonished to find Christmas came after all. Someone put a bag of Christmas presents together and put it on the porch for us. We got several board games and a huge fruit and candy basket. We giggled and laughed and squealed as we found each item in the bag. Lanny even got his own football! We were buzzing like bees, just hopping with joy. We couldn't believe someone would do this for us. Lanny thought dad might have arranged something secretly and was pumped that he would do this for us. Lola thought maybe it was our neighbor, Mr. Freedman. When we looked back out the window, we didn't see anyone. No car. No person. No one. It was a true Christmas miracle!

Christian and I found a Mr. Potato head and opened him up and all his parts. We also got Monopoly, Life, and Battleship. We even got a set of special cards called *Uno*. We read all the directions for all the games so no one could cheat. I loved to be the banker on Monopoly. I loved being the little dog. Christian would get bored and would color in the coloring books and crayons that were also in the bag. We played every game, multiple times. We played so late and so long my eyes were hot and burning with a desire to sleep. We had fresh fruit, Christmas candies, and stockings. There were little puzzles and a ball and jacks and other little tinker toys in the stockings. We couldn't believe it. We even had a little Christmas tree in a box that was just as big as Christian. We had some Christmas lights, little bulbs, and an angel for the treetop. It was a little boy angel and we called him Andrew. He came for Christmas after all.

We were so happy to put up that tree even though we didn't have electric to plug it in. Our family played and played while dad slept and slept. He never woke for Christmas. He was sick again. He would get into these states off and on between busting his ass working, and then in bed for days. While we were off school on break, he was in his sad state. Maybe her birthday triggered his sadness. He told us he was going to try to get mom to come see us for a visit which is why we thought maybe she was at the door.

As with all things abnormal, he did reach out to her and told her where we were.  After a day's drive, she arrived in Louisiana. Dad had her meet him at a hotel and asked her for sex as a requirement to get to see the kids. She told him she didn't want to take him up on his offer as she had her newborn son with her in the car.  He told her he changed his mind then.  He spat in her face and told her she got exactly what she wanted.  A replacement for Andrew, a little boy all her own. He said the kids are perfectly fine without her, and he didn't want to confuse us by having her show up after all these months.  He especially didn't want her showing up with a fucking baby.  She said she wanted to see her kids anyway.  He said no, and he got back in his truck and drove off.  She followed him in her car.

No one knows if he ever intended to let her see us.  But he got home in a frenzy and told us to hurry up and get in the truck immediately. We all jumped up and ran with him to get in the truck not knowing what we were running for or from.  While we were pulling away, we saw a big brown station wagon pull up behind us in the street.  When the car door opened, we saw mom step out and start running after our truck.  We were so confused by what was going on.  It seemed like she was mad.  Why was she running?  Why were we running? Did she come to visit us?  We had no clue.  But dad said we had to go. So, we had to go. He seemed like he was in a panic. So, we were in a panic.

We laid in the bed of the truck with our camping blankets and pillows.  The truck had a cap on top.  And we just drove and drove. I looked out the little rectangle window watching us pass cloud after cloud. I always wondered which cloud Andrew lived in. We didn't really know what heaven was, except up in the sky, and we assumed that's where you go when you die.  We thought Andrew lived in the clouds watching over us. We didn't spend much time in church, except when our neighbors on Magnolia Street, Mr. and Mrs. Young, would take us to Sunday school. Mrs. Young liked me to wear shoes, and I always seemed to show up without any shoes on. One of those days, I had shoes on with a hole in them, so Mrs. Young didn't sigh at me. So, she still stopped and bought me a pair of shoes for church. They were cheap little pink plastic jelly shoes, and I loved them. When I got home with those shoes that day, mom beat my ass with a ruler because she said I must have made Mrs. Young (who was actually a little old lady) feel sorry for me and buy me shoes. I told her mine had a hole in them. She was mostly mad because I didn't keep my shoes with the hole in them and threw them away. She threw away my little pink jellies and I found an old pair of sandals to wear instead.

Laying in the bed of this truck, we seemed to drive for a very long time. If dad was trying to lose mom, he must have done that by now. We were starting to get hungry and had to pee. But, when it turned dark, we realized we weren't just driving around. We weren't going back. We didn't know where we were going next. We were all sad that we left behind our Christmas in a bag. My new brush. My writing journal. And we left our angel. We just sunk lower and were feeling pretty glum laying in the truck bed waiting to see what was in store for us next. I also left behind Mrs. Smith, who I secretly thought was behind the Christmas bag. I never told my brothers or sister about my Christmas list. And I never got to go back to school and thank her. My heart beat hard in my throat, and I choked back the urge to cry.

We ended up in Florida at a hotel for a few weeks. Dad would leave during the day, looking for a job, and he found one. At night he would go out to the bar where he was looking for a lady friend, and he found one of those too. We didn't stay in this town long before we were on another road trip to this lady's sister's house. That was a long hot drive in the sun. We were all pissed off and steaming about not knowing what was going on. I was more upset that I was missing school. We didn't want to hang out with this family and asked dad to please go somewhere else. When it was time to leave, the girlfriend of one week stayed behind. So, it was just us 4 kids, a truck, no money, no mom, and no home. Dad found work at a construction site of a new home being built. He worked on the home, and we helped as much as we could. We set up a camp around the truck in the unfinished yard. We had campfires, hot dogs, marshmallows, Vienna sausages, and sardines for several weeks until PAYDAY!

We were so excited as we were promised dinner and a movie. We argued and argued over exactly where we would be eating. We settled on an all-you-can-eat buffet. 4 hungry kids and a hungry father. Sounds like a terrible idea. We all cleaned up as best we could and got ready to go tear up that buffet. When dad started the truck to pull out of our camping spot, the tires were just spinning and spinning, throwing sand everywhere. It seemed like we were stuck, and Christian started to cry, and dad started to yell. We rallied as a team and got some wood from the construction site to put under the tires to try to get out of the hole. And we pushed and rocked the truck and pushed, and by now we were all sweating and pissed off and dirty. But the tires finally caught on the wood and the truck started moving. We jumped in the truck and headed out, dirty and sweaty and hungrier than ever.

When we finally got to the buffet, it was dark out. We ate and ate and ate everything we could get our hands on that came around that turntable of delight. We literally stuffed our faces. Christian was the first to complain of a stomach-ache. So, we decided it was time to leave. When we reached the parking lot, of course, I puked. As I said, story of my life. Expelling bodily fluids has become a part of my lifestyle. The smell of my puke made my dad puke. I never felt so disappointed to not get a chance to digest all that good food. I remember staring at the puddle of puke, and I could make out exactly what I just wasted in the Duff's parking lot. Specifically, I regretted missing out on all the fried okra I ate. I literally contemplated picking up the pieces of okra out of the puke and eating it. I was never so disappointed in losing a meal in this way and it was heartbreaking to me to leave it in the parking lot, even though it was barf. It was at that moment in my life I understood why dogs immediately eat their puke after they puke. I thought about doing it longer than a normal child should. We never made it to the movies. And we were sad to not get to the movies since we have never been to a movie theatre yet. We also never made it back to the construction site. My dad got a hotel room around the corner from Duff's, and we slept like Kings and Queens. Finally, air conditioning... but I was hungry again!

Being hungry is an awful feeling. The aches start slowly and eventually become sharp stabs in the gut. The low growls become bellowing howls for food. To know my belly is empty is a hollow feeling. My stomach would ache so bad it would make my mouth water. When my mouth would water from this ache, it was the kind of mouthwatering that comes before you throw up. And I would try to swallow it down and breathe slow and tell myself to concentrate to help control the urge to puke. It didn't always work. I would often throw up foul tasting, yellow, slimy stomach juices. At least that was one puke I never thought about eating. To this day, hunger pains are something I struggle with as an adult. I feel taken right back to the days as a hungry child every time my stomach growls. Having food in the home is something I would never take for granted. Struggling to make ends meet is a terrible position to be in. The pain of a parent in not being able to feed your child regularly must be a devastating feeling. Almost as devastating as feeling hungry.

Roaming around all day playing in the yard and being hungry was a normal occurrence for us. Some neighbors would feed us, but we couldn't take advantage of them all the time. We would find little clover-looking plants in the yard in between the blades of grass and were ecstatic to find that they had a good flavor to them. It wasn't that they were "good good," but that they had a little bit of flavor that wasn't gross. It was edible to us, so we ate it. We would literally eat them out of the yard every chance we had. They were easy to spot with the dainty yellow flowers on top. But the most exciting thing was when you found a bunch of them in the grass, and they had small, green banana-shaped growths on them. Those tiny bananas were packed with a sour flavor, and to us, it was delicious. We never got sick, so we always made sure we ate it when we could find it. After all, we were just doing what we thought was normal. Eating grass from the yard. We thought everyone did that.

I missed about a month of third grade during our Florida excursion. We moved around from Louisiana, Florida, Virginia, and Maryland during third and fourth grade. We also ended up back in Texas. All short stops. All new friends. All new schools. I can't explain the miracle or even understand why or how, but my dad made sure we went to school. Although we did have an extended Christmas vacation, we got back into school, and I made sure I didn't skip a beat. I think we were moving around so that mom wouldn't know where we were. I think she stayed in the little house in Texas, but we didn't know where she was for sure either. We didn't know if she was really looking for us. Maybe we had to keep moving as a way to keep him from going back to her to torment her or to taunt her. Or to keep her from kidnapping us. We didn't know anything.

Once we left Florida, we ended up in a new school in Virginia. We stayed in an abandoned home. We really loved those. It was cheap. One night, Lanny, Lola, and I were sleeping in one bed. Dad was sleeping in another room with Christian. I hated it when someone touched me when I was sleeping. I hated sharing a bed with anyone. But I especially hated it when someone touched my leg with their feet. And on this night, someone kept putting their leg over mine. I would kick it off. But they kept doing it. Lanny and Lola made me sleep in the middle which led to lots of whining and kicking. One or both of them kept touching my leg with their feet or trying to lay their leg over mine. Finally, I had had enough of them, and I whined loud enough that my dad told me to come lay with him and Christian. After I jumped out of the bed, I heard a thud on the floor. When I looked to see what it was, I saw a huge snake slither into the closet. Screams ensued from every one of us and I had the heebie jeebies. The fucking snake was in the bed with us, and I was convinced that the snake was the one wrapping itself around my leg. Ew ew. I still shudder at the thought. The boys investigated the hole in the closet leading into the basement which I was told was infested with snakes. In my little girl head, I imagined boas and pythons and rattlesnakes coiled all over and hanging from the rafters. In reality, there was probably only one snake. My dad tended to over-exaggerate, which is where I get my skill. I didn't make any friends, and I didn't talk to any teachers. I just did my work quietly and didn't want to get attached to or involved in anything.

We finished up the school year and spent the summer camping in the truck all over. It was fun when we stopped at places by the water. We would go fishing and swimming. I loved catching frogs and learning how to do cannon balls. We got really good at cooking on the campfire. We had a big pot for stews, and dad would make campfire chili. It was so good on hotdogs. We stayed warm at night with our new sleeping bags. We also had a tent. Some of us stayed in the tent and whoever slept in the truck had to listen to dad snoring or farting all night.

Maryland is where my dad's oldest brother, Dale, still lived.  We showed up at his super nice condo first, and he refused to open the door for us. Dale and dad didn't have a close relationship at all.  We then went to Dale's ex-wife's home, Aunt Ann, where we were permitted to over-stay our welcome.  Dale lived in an upscale neighborhood just outside of Washington, D.C. and had left his family high and dry.  He was successful financially but had no interest in giving a single hand out.  Not to his ex-wife and children, and certainly not to us. Uncle Dale was a producer of a popular news show in D.C. Uncle Dale had 5 children: 3 boys and 2 girls. The girls were about the same ages as Lola and me. We were enrolled in a new school for the start of $4^{th}$ grade.

At school, when asked where I lived, and I mentioned all the states we have been in, everyone just assumed my dad was in the military.  It was a better reason than the truth about all the moving around, so I just let them believe that story.  Afterall, if history were to repeat itself, I wouldn't be here long.  We ate well and were doing pretty good while at Aunt Ann's.  This was the first time I ever ate name-brand cereal: Corn Pops and Kix. I was also the same size as my cousin who let me wear her name brand clothing.  She wore a lot of dresses, tights, and corduroy and I hated it.  We had a clean home to stay in and my older cousin, Sharon, would braid my hair every morning.  She tied ribbons in my ponytails that were like yarn but fat, fluffy yarn.  I wasn't much of a girly girl, but I have never had a mom or a mom-figure for that matter who would braid my hair, much less put ribbons in it.  Sharon was the mom of the house, as Aunt Ann wasn't around much to take care of her girls.  Sharon helped me and my cousin, Elizabeth pick out clothes, get breakfast, and made sure everyone was off to school on time.  We had a nice time in the area and going to civil war re-enactments around town. Some of the older boys were excited to hear the guns go off.

We had a visit from Aunt Gail and her son, Steven. We spent time as a family, and Aunt Gail was giving dad a stern talking to about all the moving around with us kids. Aunt Gail talked dad into coming back to Texas where all the sisters were living. She was always trying to take care of her baby brother. She loved telling us the story about when dad was little. He ran away from home and hid out back behind a tree. He brought a note to the house and asked Aunt Gail to bring him a sandwich when he got hungry, so she did. She said he was always the sweetest little boy. They loved to take care of their baby brother. And they always referred to Grandma Rose as "Mommy" in all of their stories and in talking about her.

And so, we left as abruptly as we arrived. No planning. No saying goodbye. This was the way it always was. Except, one new thing. Our older cousin, Jeff, one of Dale's boys, was coming with us. He was going to come with dad and help him on jobs. This stay in Maryland only lasted about 6 weeks. I made a friend who had just gotten a cast on her arm. And we left town the day before she got it off. I was mainly upset that I did not get to see what the after effect of wearing a cast for 6 weeks would do to an arm. I also accidentally dropped a paper clip into the cast and wanted to see it retrieved. I guess I will never know.

# CHAPTER FIVE

# The Sun

Once we left Maryland, we headed back to Texas. This time much further north near Houston, where my dad's sisters were now living. His older sister Joy, and his baby sister Jodi lived within blocks of each other. Joy was married and had 3 boys and 3 stepdaughters (former cousins). Here's a West Virginia twist: Aunt Joy's husband used to be married to my grandma Rose's baby sister and had 3 children. Essentially Uncle Joe was my grandma's brother-in-law and when Eileen died, he became my grandma's son-in-law. He married my dad's sister, my grandma's daughter, his former niece by marriage who used to babysit her cousins (his children), when she was only 17. Nevertheless, there was a large age-gap. I looked a lot like my Aunt Joy. Pale skin, dark hair, and a tiny, little nose. She was a drunk and pissed her pants every time she got drunk and got to laughing and telling stories. No, I did not inherit that talent, thankfully. We stayed in a rental house across the street from Aunt Joy. My youngest aunt, Jodi, was a pistol. She was married to the brother of my Uncle Joe, D.P. She had three boys also. Aunt Jodi had a trucker mouth, long, rowdy red hair, and a huge personality. She was barely 5 feet tall. She also loved to drink her beer. Aunt Gail lived in an apartment building where she was the manager. Her place had a swimming pool, which was the most exciting part. She had Steven and a daughter, Elizabeth, who was also close to my age. Yes, I had two cousins around my same age, and both with the same first name! We were a now a big family here in Texas, and had the support of each other. My aunts were my moms, and my dad had yet another new girlfriend. But it was also fun to have cousins my age around, my cousin Jeff, and built-in friends!

In my new school, I was eager to show my smarts on grades and tests. I asked for extra work to take home. I tested high and enjoyed hearing positive feedback from every teacher I could. I did my homework at home as soon as I could. Sometimes I did it twice just for fun. I worked ahead in workbooks. I read ahead in class work. I just wanted to fill the space in my head with the most positive energy I could, and that was learning. At our Houston school, my first day there, there was a teamwork project to build a paper airplane. Each group was given a set of supplies to build the airplane. At the end of the two-day project, each team was to then have their paper planes judged for the plane that could fly the farthest, and the highest, for example. There were 8 teams and there were 8 kids pre-selected as a team leader who were to pick teammates. As we stood in a line in the front of the class, one by one, every kid in the class was picked, until I was left standing alone. The next team was forced to have the weird, new kid join their group. It was always awkward being the new kid all the time. Most of the classmates had already established friendships every time I entered a new school. They lived by each other or knew each other's families. My cheeks would always get hot and red, and my neck and chest would get splotchy red when I was standing alone often in situations like this. It was pretty common because of all the moving around we did. I didn't feel nervous about it anymore. I would breathe in and out slowly to relax my nerves. I would also breathe in and out slowly to keep from tearing up, because I would never let any of these snide motherfuckers see me cry or know my feelings were hurt. But my face and neck turning red was involuntary and out of my control. My own body betrayed me. And I hated that for me.

I joined the team that never picked me, and we worked quickly putting together the paper airplane. No one spoke to me the first day of the project. That night I went home and tried different ways to make a plane on paper and different ideas of what other supplies to add to it. During the second day, I would shyly offer suggestions and the team would try them. We would practice outside flying the different planes. The teacher told us we would be putting a plane in for judging by the end of today, and we needed to come up with a name for our team. We used an initial from each person's last name, and with the A from Allen, we became BACHY's Bombers. The kids on my team were glad that I joined them since my initial really helped us come up with a name. When we went out for judging, our plane flew the farthest and we got a ribbon for our plane. One of the best additions to our plane was the paper clip I put on the nose. It made me think of my friend with the cast. But I made some new friends that day and finally had kids to talk to at school.

At home, we feasted. Everyone cooked or we cooked out. We had big family dinners and parties and get togethers. It was the best part. Dad and Jeff were making money and we had a nice little place to live. I even had a friend from school who lived on my street. She would sometimes come over and eat dinners with us and she would swim with me at Aunt Gail's apartments whenever we wanted to. The cousins all taught me how to play rummy and we would play card games for hours on end.  Some of the cousins also had some of the same games we left behind in Louisiana.  Playing Battleship was my favorite.  We would also dig for worms in the yard and go fishing.  We spent a lot of time just being a part of the family.  We enjoyed having family, and money, and games, and food.

At the end of the school year, there was a field day of races. I was little and fast and was excited to sign up to race some of the sprint races, and play some of the games like the water balloon toss and the sack relays.  I needed to be on a team and was able to join groups with some of my BACHY's Bombers friends.  I let everyone know how excited I was to run the sprints and that I thought I could win. Our class would be competing against the other classes from our grade.  Everyone said the fastest girl in our grade always won the sprint races and that I didn't stand a chance.  I had no idea who she was, but everyone talked about BeeBee.

Once the races were called, I headed over to the area where we needed to check in and get in the lane I was assigned for the race. When I heard BeeBee give her name, I turned to see who she was. She was a tall, skinny Mexican girl with a long braid of dark hair halfway down her back.  She had running shoes and athletic shorts.  I was wearing jean shorts bib overalls, which were the only shorts I had clean for the day's hot outdoor event.  And I had on a little pink tank top underneath.  But at least I had Christian's tennis shoes on for field day. We were lined up in lanes beside each other.  She was in lane 1, and I was in lane 2. We were running the 200-meter dash. It is half the track. I always felt like I could run for days, but I really wasn't sure if I was fast or not.  Once the race started, BeeBee's starting line was behind me.  I just took off and ran as fast as I could. I could hear her right behind me all the way until we got to the curve of the track.  And there is where the staggered starting line evens everyone out and she was right beside me. I didn't see anyone in the other lanes. I was trying to stay in step with her as much as I could. Our feet were hitting the ground in sync. But with her long legs, she was able to stride out and pull ahead towards the end of the race to win. And I came in second. And everyone else was not even close. My BACHY's Bombers friends were jumping up and down and were cheering so loud for me. BeeBee walked up to me and said, "Good race, new girl. It's about time I got a little competition." I was so happy to get the 2nd place ribbon during the announcement ceremony at the end of the field day. I was so excited for the end of school and summer and really hoped I would see my friends from the BACHY's Bombers, and BeeBee the next school year. But of course, that was wishful thinking.

Over the summer, my dad and his new girlfriend got married. And once again, we moved. Jeff went back to Maryland. And now we had an extra kid. Beth's son was around the same age as Lola. He spent the summer with his dad in Ohio and came back to live with his mom. She had another kid Lanny's age, but she didn't want to move with her mom and chose to stay in Ohio with her dad. Our new place was by the water. We spent that summer fishing, crabbing, shrimping, and playing on the beach. At this house on stilts on Knickerbocker Street, I got the best summer tan on my back. I had an eternal tan line on my back for two summers straight from spending every day in the sunshine. I spent all day every day leaning over the water rolling in with my back facing the sun waiting for a school of minnows to swim by the shoreline. Then I would scoop them in my hands and throw them up on the sand. Christian would put them in the bucket for bait to fish at night. We would wade out across the water and swim and fish and crab. It was the best summer we ever had, where we could cook what we ate and had so much fun doing it. One day, Lanny caught an enormous shrimp while we were all standing closer to the highway. While he was holding it up, a passerby slowed down to take a look at it and bought it off him. It was probably frowned upon for us to have been out in the water as far as we were, and we certainly had no business up by South Padre Island Drive unsupervised.

While the beach days were fun, they were also dangerous without adult supervision. We were spending all our time in the Gulf of Mexico. During one of our fishing incidents, Lanny almost had his fingernail bit off by what I presume was a dogfish. At least that is what we called it. My new teenage stepbrother split his foot wide open on a seashell so deep we could see tendons. Christian split his head open jumping on the bed trying to do flips while we jammed some loud Van Halen songs. We really liked to listen to the song Jamie's Cryin'. We had some really loud speakers. We also spent time making up games to play out of boredom. We played a game called prisoner. We had to try to find ways to escape the room we were locked in. During one of the games, I found it too easy that the door was unlocked, so I opened it and peeked out to see where the guards were. Once I peeked my head out, my sister threw a wooden brush towards the door across the room and hit me right smack dab in the middle of the forehead. I damn near passed out. Lola was so scared, she thought she killed me. When the hazy view from my eyes became clearer, I could see her standing over me sobbing. And I saw something else sitting on my forehead. I reached up to try to wipe it off my head. But it didn't wipe off. In fact, it hurt. Bad. It was the biggest goose egg I have ever seen. It was making me go cross-eyed because I could literally see it when I looked up. But don't worry. We put some ice on that shit, and I wasn't allowed to play prisoner anymore. Everyone was mad at me for ruining the game. It seems Christian or I would always get hurt doing something. It was annoying being the babies in the family. We decided not to tell dad.

Instead, we headed down to the beach where we played a game of war. We built bunkers and made balls of sand to throw at our enemy. We had to get creative. We had to dig down far enough to hit water. We needed wet sand to pack our sand balls together. We spent most of the time creating a bunker, and once we were "ready," it was time for war. We always found a way to make it as dangerous as possible. We would add a shell, sticks, or a piece of glass in the center to make sure we made an impact. As many times as we aimed for faces, we were lucky we were all terrible at throwing. And we are lucky we all survived with both eyeballs!

I was never too sure where dad was or our stepmom, Beth. I don't know if she worked or if they were working on drywall together, but they were gone a lot. There was a bar between our rental house and the water. Sometimes the barmaids would give us cold pops and water when we were out fishing and playing in the water all day. I also spent a lot of time looking through the trash for any good food they were throwing away. One of the days, dad was gone from pretty much sun up to sun down. We crabbed all day long with our crab traps. We put water in a trash can and filled it up with as many blue crabs as we could catch. When dad came home late that night, he was tickled pink. We had a huge crab boil and ate and ate and ate crab until I was sick. But that didn't stop me from eating more. It was our all-time favorite. They didn't come in close enough to shore for us very often, but when they did and we could catch them, we would get a lot. I had butter dripping down my chin and ate like there was no tomorrow.

That summer we were between the ages of 7 and 13, and there were now 5 of us. A fun addition to the mix besides all the childhood injuries, was the new stepmom that liked to drink. One time, she jumped down the front flight of stairs of our little house on stilts. I mean, we jumped down those stairs for fun. She jumped for drunk. We would put a mattress at the bottom and bet who would jump from the highest step without dying. I think that was the actual requirement. We loved to compete and apparently, we loved to injure ourselves as well. I jumped from so high up that when I landed, my legs buckled, and my chin hit the top of my knee. My teeth clanked together so hard I thought they might fall out. I didn't win and I didn't jump again, as I didn't want to knock my own teeth out. But I also knocked my own breath out and struggled to catch it. I played it off like I wasn't hurt because I didn't want anyone to get mad at me for ruining another game. I just walked off to the water to sit and dip my toes in while the sun set behind the interstate. It was the most beautiful place I have ever seen, and I hoped and hoped we never ever left this place.

Some days I would sit at the water by myself, and some days Christian would come sit with me. We would make little holes and fill them with water like our own little swimming pools. The interstate to South Padre went as far as we could see, and so did the water. We always talked about swimming to the "island". But we didn't want to get stranded on the wrong island like *Gilligan's Island*. It was fun to think about what was across the water, but we never made a trip to South Padre Island. Thankfully, we never tried to swim it either. One of the days at the water daydreaming, I made myself a little bed in the sand with a pillow and carved out a place for my butt and fell asleep. I woke up to fluttering by my face and a seagull standing by my head looking down at my face. I think he was checking to see if I was alive. I freaked out and screamed and he flew off. I don't know how long I was sleeping, but when I got home no one was there. It was starting to get dark, and I just sat by myself waiting for everyone to get back home for hours.  Turns out, they left to go out to eat and I missed out because I was nowhere to be found. I was ok with that since I would rather have some peace and quiet at the beach.  And I would nap by the beach instead of eating any day of the week.

As it turns out, dad struggled to get along with drunk Beth.  They also liked to argue quite a bit, and they were usually both drunk. On one occasion, she came barreling in the house screaming and yelling asking where dad was.  She was holding a shot gun pointed down at her side and her eyes were wide and crazy-looking.  She found him in the bathroom where he was taking a shower. She started pushing and shoving him and was screaming at the top of her lungs for help. Dad jumped out of the shower, wet and naked, with the water still running. He grabbed a towel, and she raised the gun and was pointing it in his face, and he dropped his towel and put his hands up.  We all took off running and locked ourselves in our room.  She was chasing my dad around while he was running from her naked.  She was yelling at him about some whore he was flirting with at the bar next door. He got into their bedroom and was able to shut the door before she got in. She was banging on the door with the gun, and we could tell she was hammered.  She kept screaming off and on, "Help! Help me!" maybe hoping the neighbors would call the cops.

Dad kept telling her she was scaring the kids. So, she came over to our door and put her face near the crack and asked in a sarcastic tone, "Are you kids scared? Like really scared, guys?" While slurring her speech in a super slow pattern, she then kept repeating, "The gun ain't even loaded guys. It ain't even loaded.  Like for real."  She was clearly hammered, and we were hoping what she said was true.  She kept going back and forth to each door.  She would say things like "Nobody even likes me." "You guys don't even like me." Eventually, it got really quiet. We peeked out the door and saw dad peeking out the door, too. It felt like our prisoner game all over again, but in real life. She was passed out sleeping on the couch with her head leaned all the way back and her mouth wide open. She had the gun on her lap. Dad took it off her lap and told us to just go to bed. I don't know what he did with the gun. I never saw a gun in the house before that, and I never saw one again.

We actually thought Beth was mean and didn't really spend time with us or talk to us very much. I didn't like her and none of us had any plans to be nice to her. She said "like" all the time and "really" and most of the time she slurred her words. She was always very sarcastic to us and referred to us as "guys" all the time. It was annoying. Most of the time, we could tell she was annoyed with us. She would always raise her screeching voice up a notch when she caught us goofing off and not cleaning our room or the kitchen. She likes to get right in your face to speak to you and with her drunken slur, she spit her words on your face. She also liked to put her finger right on your cheek to make a point. She tried this a few times with Lola, but Lola slapped her hand away several times. As someone who doesn't take any shit, Lola was not to be fucked with. Beth learned that rather quickly. Lola was eye to eye with her letting her know she would gladly knock her on her ass if she did it again. And she meant it. She stopped doing it with her but made it a point to do it to Christian and me in front of her just to aggravate things.

The new stepbrother, Jay, was ok overall. But he was whiny and needy. I hated the way he flipped his surfer-looking hair. He was spoiled and a bit of a sissy. It was annoying to watch her do everything for only him. Make him a plate. Cut up his steak. Take him to the store. Take him to the laundromat. They would only wash her clothes and his clothes. We were used to doing everything for ourselves. But she didn't try to bond to us or spend any time with any of us or do anything for us. We were fine with that.

Beth didn't like us staying at the little beach house since there was a whore at the bar next door. I guess to keep from fighting, Beth put her foot down and said either she was moving out or we were all moving. So, we had to move. I was completely heart-broken and pissed off at her for making us move. We went from the beach to an apartment. There were lots of kids and families which was actually pretty nice. It was right up the road from the new school in Flour Bluff, where my aunts were now living again. It was time to make new friends. Again. And it was time to expect to be picked last. Again. But school is school. At least I enjoyed getting a new classroom. One of the best parts of this school was that there wasn't just one classroom. Each classroom was divided into 4 sections, and we moved from section to section for different classes. The worst part of this school was that the kids who paid for their lunch would form one line, and the poor kids who got free lunch would get into another line. I knew being in this line automatically changed who my friends would be. I decided at this point that I didn't need to make friends, since I doubted we would be living here very long anyway,

My favorite teacher at this school was easy to find. My English teacher, Mrs. Woodruff was the best one ever. She quickly caught on to my accelerated rate of learning. She would call on me the most and praise me for doing the work and knowing the work. She took an interest in me and made it a point to say the nicest things ever. Although she was an overall nice teacher, it really started sinking in with the way she spoke and the extra praise she would give. I loved it when she would say, "What a brain!" or "You might outsmart me yet." Mrs. Woodruff was a little older with fluffy white hair. She often wore two barrettes, one on each side, to keep her hair out of her face. When she wasn't wearing those barrettes, she would blow a puff of air from her bottom lip to move her hair out of her eyes when she was talking. She would always do a little happy dance when someone was giving a good answer. I loved to make her do the happy dance. She was so cute when she did it. She enjoyed teaching and it showed.

She would give me extra assignments and different projects to work on whenever I asked for more. She also sent me to do some testing. She said it was so I could get better work to do. We had a big school and all of us kids were at the same place for a change. This school had an elementary and middle school at the same location. I loved walking outside after school and finding my brothers and my sister to walk home. Lanny didn't appreciate us following along since he was older, but we didn't care. It was a short walk to the apartments, and we walked with the group of kids who all lived in the same place. This school had a huge outdoor area and playground. We played kickball and could also watch our older cousins playing baseball for the Hornets. It seemed like we always had something going on during the school day and things at home were settling down.

A few months ticked by before we knew it, and my teacher asked me to take a note home to my mom. She wanted to set up a conference. I told her I would bring the note home. Dad did set up a meeting and Mrs. Woodruff and a bunch of other people were there to go over my test results. I wasn't super happy about missing my other classes for this conference. Dad walked in and sat by me, and we chatted for a little bit during the awkward silence. Everyone kept staring across the table as if waiting for my dad to start the meeting they scheduled. Finally, one of the other teachers asked if we were just waiting for "mom". Dad said quickly, "There is no mom. Just me." The teachers looked at me with pity. They went over my scores and showed a comparison to kids in my grade in my school, and comparison to kids in my grade in the state.  On each chart there was an area to show acceptable performance levels in many different subjects.  It looked like a stop light.  In yellow areas, it was average.  In the top color of green, was exceptional.  They had to point to the line at the top of the green section to show where my scores fell, since each one was the line at the top of the section.  The only one not at the top was Science.  That was supposed to show that my scores were off the charts for the most part, not just for my school, but for all kids in my grade in Texas.

In the meeting, my dad would look over at me and smile while they explained score after score.  And then they said the purpose of the meeting was to ask my dad to consider moving me up into the next grade level. The scores compared to my grade level were astronomical. In fact, most of them were showing me scoring at nearly 3 grade levels above my own.  They kept saying, "April is gifted." Dad said he knew I was smart, but he had no idea I was that smart.  He also said he would never consider doing that.  He was asked by Mrs. Woodruff to take a day to consider it so that I could be at a level where I could be challenged.  He said he did not need any time to consider it, as he would never approve it.  The biggest issue keeping me in the grade I am in is that my sister is in the grade above me.  He did not feel this would be a good idea for us to share a class and friends.  And, he also said the other worry is that I am so small.  He didn't feel it would be fair to put me in a class of bigger and older kids.  I had no idea what it all meant to be gifted and I had no idea why they felt I should skip a grade. I was just hoping Mrs. Woodruff would be allowed to keep giving me more work. She promised she would still do that.

At home at the apartment, we didn't have a beach, but we did have a swimming pool.  Well, we didn't really have a swimming pool. The apartment complex behind us had a pool and we would sneak in there by climbing the fence.  And we would get kicked out all the time.

But that didn't stop us from enjoying the ten minutes or 2 hours we were under the radar.  Most of the time we were kicked out because Christian was not a good swimmer and would draw attention to us when we would swim in the deep end without him.  He would cry in the shallow end and cause a scene until they noticed he was with just us and not with parents.  And then someone would always chime in and say we don't even live there.   On warm weekends we would get in the truck and drive to the beach where we spent the whole day without Beth. She hated the beach. She hated the sand.  And we liked spending time without her!

Beach days consisted of jumping in the waves and fishing from the shore.  My cousins that lived in the same town would all jump in the back of dad's truck and go to the beach with us. Every cousin we ever had around loved their Uncle Lanny.  He could make massive meals for lots of people.  He was funny and a prankster.  He was the kind of "pull my finger" uncle.  He loved to tell jokes and always had the kids laughing and giggling. We spent the days as a family in the sunshine on the beach.  We would explore the sand dunes and just be beach bums all day. We just had to be careful of the rattlesnakes hiding under rocks.

At school, I excelled.  At home, turmoil was always brewing.  During another one of their fights, Beth jumped out of the second-story window at our apartment building and landed on the air conditioning unit outside.  We had to call the ambulance and the cops came too. She was gone for a few days.  We didn't go see her and didn't miss her or care. I was hoping she wouldn't come back.  But her son was still with us.  I would just want her to come back and get him, and that was it. But, after a few days, she was back like nothing ever happened.  She was all smiles and in a good mood, which was creepy. Beth made me my very first birthday cake ever.  Christian and I had birthdays 4 days apart right around Easter that year.  The cake was my dad's favorite flavor, German Chocolate.  Christian turned 8 and I was turning 10.  The cake was awesome.  I was in awe.  It was shaped like a train, connected with licorice, and gum drops for head lights.  I got a baton for my birthday.  It was a little girly for me, but I could whack the shit out of my little brother with it when I needed to!  Beth could bake.  She also made a cake at Easter, with green colored coconut in the shape of a Rabbit.  We made this apartment our home.  We had actual beds and bedrooms, and furniture and food.  But we still had chaos.  It just loved to follow us around from place to place.

I went to school and rotated to my English class and there was a substitute teacher.  Another lady came in our class and then started to open the class dividers and asked the students from all 4 sections to come to the middle for a discussion.  She told us that Mrs. Woodruff passed away the night before.  My heart blinked away some tears.  My throat closed a little and I didn't breathe for it seemed like a whole minute.  I blinked a lot to make sure I didn't cry.  But I was crying inside, and I was terribly sad for my favorite teacher.  They told us how she died.  What they explained to us was that it was an aneurism.  What I heard as a 10-year-old child was that a blood vessel broke open in her head and the bleeding is what caused her to die.  She had a vein in the middle of her eyebrows that would bulge out when she was mad at the disruptive kids in the class. My gifted brain heard these things and imagined that vein popped out of her head and dripped all her blood out on her book she was probably reading at home in her rocking chair.  I had no idea what they were talking about and would have to look these things up when I got home and learn about it.

We had a school counselor come talk to us about how we felt and made sure to answer any questions we had.  I didn't want to talk to the counselor as I always felt the last one was too nosey and asked too many questions about my life. The class was allowed to go to Mrs. Woodruff's service a few days later and meet her family. I was so scared to see a dead body, but we were all assured there would not be any body. There was a memorial vase, and they had her burned up and put in there. How disgusting! We were allowed to walk in a line, shaking hands with her family members, sign our name on a guest book, and then leave. Mrs. Woodruff's daughter came to thank us for coming before we loaded back onto the busses. She asked, "Which one of you is April?" I raised my hand and said that was me. She handed me a book. She said her mom went on and on and talked about me and how smart I was. She said her mom had a ton of books and she just wanted to give me one of them. This was a book by Judy Blume called, "Tales of a Fourth Grade Nothing." I thanked her for the book and opened it quick and flipped the pages to make sure there wasn't any blood on it. It was just a book, but it meant the world to me. My eyes almost cried. I couldn't wait to get home and read it. Alone in my room, tears were welling up in my eyes thinking how proud Mrs. Woodruff was of me. I couldn't remember a time someone really expressed being proud of me. The suck up. The annoying brat who knew all the answers. The poor kid. The motherless kid who moved all the time. The kid who wore the same clothes every day. The kid with one pair of shoes. The kid with freckles and one dimple and a himple. All these things described me. I wasn't anything I felt such a smart lady, a teacher, should be proud of. But for the first time ever, I felt a little pang self-worth welling up in my head, and at the same time, my tiny little heart stung with another loss.

I had to breathe in and out slowly to keep the tears from dripping out. I didn't like to feel sad or cry. I didn't like people to see me cry and think I was weak and small. I pinched the side of my leg really hard to keep from crying a lot. I was already puny; I already saw myself as weak.

I didn't want to add to it.  I couldn't believe I would never see Mrs. Woodruff again.  I would never have her pulling me aside to ask me how my day was.  She always had peppermint candies in her pocket, just for me.  But nothing in this life or world was ever just for me. And nothing lasted forever.  Losing my favorite teacher I had only known for a few short months, was just another reminder.  And I would be fine. I always was. You just get used to losing things, even if that meant people.

# CHAPTER SIX

# The Rain

For Halloween, we did our first trick-or-treat ever around the apartment complex. We dressed up like ghosts with whatever white clothing and towels we could put together to make us a costume. One of the apartments we went to said we were cute mummies. So that was close enough. In these times, we lived in fear of razor blades being put in our candy and we were only allowed to trick-or-treat in the day light. Beth had to inspect our candy first. Then dad had to inspect it for the best candies, and then we got the rest. We would trade each other for the best ones. I hated the chocolate and would trade for any hard candies. We made lots of friends in the apartment complex. We played music and would have dance parties in the gang way of our apartment with the kids from the upstairs apartment. I didn't know for sure what everyone else called it, but the gang way was the center area or breezeway where the staircase was for the upstairs apartments and where the doorways were for the downstairs apartments. That was where everyone would store their bikes. But that Halloween, we got more than candy that day. We got to pack up and move. The end of the month seemed to be the best time to move. And it probably had to do with not paying rent. This came as no surprise to any of us.

I didn't care if we moved. I especially didn't care anymore with Mrs. Woodruff being gone. I didn't care about going to school if she wasn't there anyway. It's like she left me. She was the one who moved away first! How dare she. The worst part about it was that we were going back to Ohio. Beth missed her daughter and wanted to be closer to her. Moving again was getting old. We moved to a town called Castalia in a trailer park until my dad could find us a house big enough for all of us. We were all crammed in a small trailer. I kept my book from Mrs. Woodruff and read it during the drive from Texas to Ohio. I read it more times than I could count, and I would sleep with it under my pillow. We went to a new school again. It was so tiny compared to Flour Buff and I didn't have any friends. Again. When we got to school that first day, they were having a Halloween party in the classroom in the afternoon and the kids were all to bring a costume to change in for the afternoon. I didn't bring one because I didn't know. But dad promised he would bring me one to school before the party started, and he left.

The party started at lunch time and when it was time to go to lunch, I went to the bathroom to hide. I didn't want to be the only kid without a costume. After a few minutes a teacher came into the bathroom to get me. She said someone was at the school for me and she walked me outside to a car where my dad was holding a bag with a Halloween costume. I squealed with glee and grabbed the bag and grabbed dad's arm hanging out the door and squeezed it and kissed his arm a bunch of times and thanked him for doing this for me. I was so excited to open the package and put on my cape and wrist bands. It also had a plastic Wonder Woman face with a skinny elastic band to hold it on my face. Just a few days earlier we were trick-or-treating for the first time, and now I had my very own real costume.  I went from feeling low and defeated to pure bliss.  It wasn't very often that I had anything new or fit in or did everything all the other kids were doing.  After the lunch party, we were allowed to wear our costumes to class.  I felt so included as part of the class since there were 3 other girls with Wonder Woman costumes.  Even our teacher was dressed up.  My dad had a lot of kids to take care of, and I know we didn't have very much money, but this was one of those moments that filled up my heart to feel included.  I finished up the rest of 4$^{th}$ grade at Townsend School and it was time to move again.  Dad found us a house.

We moved back to the teeny, tiny town of Bellevue and we were right back to where we started.  Dad rented us a big house and it even had a nice yard and a greenhouse. It was right beside a church at a busy intersection.  The church was just behind our back yard.  The church parking lot was right beside us and we parked our car in the corner spot closest to the house.  Just on the other side of the parking lot was the overpass. We spent the summer visiting Grandma Rose and getting our new house set up.  I loved hearing the church bells on the weekends.  Even though we lived this close to the church, we still never went.

I started 5th grade in Bellevue in the fall. I maintained good grades and never fell behind in any of my work. But in all the moving, I lost my Judy Blume book. I looked in every box, in every container of anything I could find.  It was just gone. I was heartbroken. Every time I saw it available for purchase on the scholastic book order form, I could never get it as we never had any money to buy any books. I gave up asking for it.  As dad would say, "You should have taken care of the one you had." Secretly, I thought he purposely lost it or got rid of it like Andrew's little box.  But I could never prove it.  I was just sad about it.

All of us kids were overall good students. Christian struggled the most with schoolwork. The night before our first day of school, Lola and I were laying in our shared bed while Dad was blaring music downstairs. We were giggling and sharing all the Spanish cuss words we knew. Lola said, "I wonder if our teacher would know what *puta* means." And we laughed thinking about saying that word at school. Just then, Dad was standing in the doorway and overheard what we said. He told us, "Yes. Your teachers will know if you are saying bad words in Spanish. Go to bed potty mouths." He scared us into not saying our Spanish cuss words at school since we didn't want to get in trouble.

We were better at getting ourselves to school on time. Even if that meant we had to jump the train to get to school. There is a train track between us and our school we had to cross to get there. As always with this damn town the trains were stopped on the tracks, but it was worse when we were trying to get to school. So, we had a habit of throwing our stuff over the section between the train cars and climbing up and over there. On one of the occasions, I had to throw my clarinet to the other side and hope it didn't break. Thankfully it did not. And on one occasion, I was last to go over, and the train jerked. I almost fell off in between the cars. After that, I was scared to cross over and waited for the train the next time it stopped, and I was late to school.

At school Lola and I were thick as thieves. We would find each other at recess and play. One of those days, everyone was picking kids to be on a kick ball team. Lola was the one picking, and I was excited because I knew she would never let me be picked last. In fact, she picked me first. I felt like I was ten feet tall for that game. She was bigger than most of the kids in her grade and I was smaller than most in mine. She was bigger than the boys even. One of the boys, was really chubby and he got mad when Lola threw him out at home plate. He started mooing at her and called her "moose." The other kids said it too, and she told him she "would rather be a moose any day than a fat ass, and you are still out." Everyone laughed at him. I think that boy would be what we call these days, a bully. He was hateful and always found a way to make fun of my sister's size. And if my sister didn't like him, I didn't like him either.

Dad struggled to find work and stay sober, and so did Beth. They also struggled to get along. She cried all the time and would tell my dad we were mean to her. I am sure we were, but it made us hate her even more. She fell down the stairs drunk again. This woman had a problem getting up and down in buildings. This time she was holding a glass of liquor and cut herself up pretty badly. Beth loved to paint, and she would let me play with her paints. It was fun and I really liked it. She showed me how she blended colors together and the different brushes she used to make different leaves and branches and clouds. She was very talented.

My dad had another great stereo system with Peavey speakers taller than me. He would have parties keeping us kids up late at night, even on school nights. We knew about liquor and pot. We could smell it at night upstairs in our rooms. We tried to drown out the sound with our own music, the Michael Jackson Thriller album that my grandma bought for Lola! One time when we came home from school, dad and his friends were sorting out their pot on the table and separating it into baggies. There was a huge bag of it still in the freezer. Dad rolled his pot up in the little white papers and told us to "take off." It was music and smoking time again. One thing we got that we didn't need, was a dog! She was a light-colored lab mix. She had blonde hair, so we named her Sandy because we also loved the movie *Grease*. Sandy wasn't allowed in the house, so when it got cold outside, we would sneak her in when dad wasn't paying attention, or he was partying with his friends. We would bring her in the basement from the cellar doors outside. We had a washer and dryer in the basement. And we had a laundry chute from upstairs. Sandy would lay on the pile of laundry in the middle of the floor. It was a perfect set up.

One day it was snowing and really cold outside, and Sandy was barking non-stop at the back door. Dad was yelling at her constantly. She was panting and pacing at the back door, which was something she normally didn't do. She had a little doghouse and some straw by the back door, but she just wouldn't go in it. Dad wouldn't let us bring her in no matter how many times we asked. I went into the basement with Lanny to try to open the cellar doors, but they wouldn't open. We thought they might be frozen because of the cold so we ran upstairs to look outside and noticed someone had put a combination lock on the doors and we couldn't open them. Dad must have figured out we let Sandy in the house that way or to be safe, he just wanted to keep those doors locked. Either way, Sandy barked for what seemed like hours at the door, until it stopped.

The next morning, I went out to feed and water Sandy, and noticed she wasn't in her house. I wandered around the yard until I found her laying on the cellar doors. She had never done that. She was in a tight little circle and when she awoke, I noticed she had two little puppies laying underneath her. It was so cold out and they were so tiny and wet, they were frozen to the door. I yelled for Lanny and Lola to come help. We had to use warm water to get them unstuck from the doors. We grabbed some towels and snuck Sandy in the house through the back door and led her into the basement. She was still panting and breathing funny. And just then she had a little puppy on the pile of laundry. We tried to warm up the two frozen pups with warm towels from the dryer, but they were obviously dead. The new puppy was also not breathing or moving. Sandy was licking it and seemed like she was trying to get it to wake up. But it wasn't moving. We went to get some water for Sandy and bring her food in the basement and to make sure dad and Beth were gone so we didn't get in any trouble. When we got back to the basement, the new puppy was gone. And the two dead puppies were still wrapped in their towel. When we realized Sandy must have eaten her puppy, we were disgusted. And before she could eat the two frozen ones, we took them outside and buried them in the back flower garden by the church. We made a little cross with sticks and string and said what little we knew about a prayer.

Sandy loved to go with us to pick blackberries. We would grab buckets and ladders and head out to the country to a farm area where dad's friends lived near-by. Sandy would eat the berries we dropped and run up and down the ruts in the field. She would head into the woods chasing rabbits but would never go too far for too long out of our site. She loved to run around chasing us kids and would jump up to knock us over and lick our faces. A lot of the time, while we all went from tree to tree, Christian would lay on Sandy watching us for hours. When we got home with the buckets of berries, we would help Beth get them washed up and she would make all kinds of sweet goodies with them. My favorite was blackberry jam. It was so good on toast. Lanny hated it because he didn't like the seeds.

Eventually, Beth was just gone and so were her things. She stopped being there and we hardly noticed. We were used to not having a mother in the home. We were getting better at getting to school on time. I had a friend, Angela, who lived right down the road from me. She was loud and silly, and I was quiet and shy for the time being. Angela was Hispanic too, although she actually looked like it. I didn't. Her mom was short and cute and sweet. But she was stern with Angela. Her mom also only had one leg, and one of her legs was a prosthetic. It was fascinating as I have never seen anyone with a limb missing, let alone a fake leg. Not having a leg didn't stop her from driving or working or cooking. She was always in Angela's business and asked a million questions about where she was going and what she was doing. She liked to feed me. And I liked to be fed, so that was something I liked. She made Mexican food and tamales. It was delicious. Christian also had a friend on the other side of the overpass. They spent every single day together, playing any kind of ball game you can think of. They were inseparable. Paul was way taller than Christian, and they looked like David and Goliath standing beside each other. He was a sweet kid who spoke with a bit of a lisp. But so did Christian. That made them two peas in a pod.

One thing we needed, and I didn't have, was a coat. My grandma lived in town and bought us all hats and gloves. We didn't need any of this in Texas. One night after a choir concert, my older brother and stepbrother came home with a boy's jacket they said someone left behind. Since no one claimed it, they brought it home. It didn't fit anyone but me. I was so happy to have a warm coat to wear to school. After a few days, I was called into the office and asked to bring the coat in with me. Another girl from the grade below me was just walking out. I went in to speak to the principle who asked me where I got my coat. When I told him the story, he said that it was considered stealing and that the coat didn't belong to me. The little girl explained she saw me wearing it and described a rust stain from their dog's chain on the sleeve, which is how she knew it was her brother's coat. When I looked down and saw the rust stain I was mortified. I handed the coat over and asked if I would be in trouble. The principle gave me extra duty and I had to clean in the cafeteria after lunch instead of recess for the rest of the week.

I told my Grandma Rose the story and I told her I was in trouble for stealing. She was upset that I got in trouble, and she bought me a silky lavender sweater, a new outfit, a pair of roller skates and a puffy blue coat from JCPenney. My outfit was the nicest new clothes I ever had! I had red jeans, and a blue shirt with puffy sleeves with white polka dots. And I loved that I had a coat of my own. Grandma Rose would just stop by and take whoever wanted to go with her for a ride. She always wanted someone to tag along to the next town over to Clyde for a filet-o-fish sandwich at McDonald's. Bellevue didn't have a McDonald's so going there with Grandma Rose down Route 20 for a 15-minute drive was a special treat. She loved doing things like that for us. She retired from GE and was the sweetest and funniest storyteller. She was our saving grace. She did her best to try to keep us fed and clothed. I know my dad would borrow money from her all the time that he never had any way or intentions of paying back. She likely knew that was going to be the case. But no matter how much money he borrowed or suckered out of her, we never had enough money for food or rent or electric on a regular basis. We were always short on money for something.

We had another family of friends who lived across the church parking lot. It turns out they were new to town. One girl, Emily, was in my grade. And another girl, Dawn, was in Lola's grade. Well, they were friends until I found Emily wearing my roller skates in the church parking lot. Normally I wouldn't care, but she kept running in the part of the parking lot that wasn't paved, and over the rocks. She said I left them out by the parking lot, so she put them on. I am pretty sure that was a lie, but I probably did leave them on the back porch, not thinking someone would come on my porch and take them and wear them without asking. I would never have the nerve to do such a thing. I asked her over and over to stop going in the rocks because it was making little dents on my big red wheels on my brand-new skates my Grandma bought for me. Sandy was running around chasing Christian as he was running around trying to chase Emily. Emily would go as fast as she could in the parking lot into the stone area and run with the skates on. She said it was fun. Finally, she skated back to where I was sitting, and took off my skates. She threw one beside me. And without warning, she threw the other one at my head and hit me in the face. Christian started chasing her, and so did Sandy. I was trying to run after her too, but I only had socks on, and it was hard stepping on the stones running across the parking lot. Plus, I was holding one eye that started to swell shut from being smashed in the face with my own skates. And of course, it started to rain. Hard. Emily ran across the parking lot and across the street to her house, and Sandy continued to follow her. Sandy crossed the street and got hit by a car right in front of us. She flew onto the side of the road and didn't move. The lady driving was putting on makeup and almost hit Emily as well. The rain was pouring so hard, I thought maybe I didn't really see what I think I just saw. But when I got closer, Sandy was laying there dead. The driver stopped for a brief second, then drove off. Emily was saying she was sorry. I wasn't sure if she was sorry for hitting me causing a big lump under my eye or if she was sorry our dog got hit by a car. It didn't matter. I never spoke to her again. I wished she was the one who got hit by a car instead of Sandy. Christian and I ran back home to tell dad what happened. He came and picked Sandy up off the side of the yard by Emily's in the pouring rain. He carried her to the bed of his truck and told us to hop in. He went and got a shovel and we drove to the blackberry trees. Dad buried Sandy in her favorite spot. We said our goodbyes and we never picked blackberries again.

Going to Grandma's house was the best place when we were feeling sad. She had the best glasses and real furniture and food. She would let me mow her lawn and help her around the house. I loved helping her and she would make me a tall glass with ice from the silver ice trays. I lost quite a few skin cells on those things getting my wet fingers stuck to them.  They had a slanted tray inside with a handle extending to the top.  You had to jiggle the handle back and forth to break the cubes free from the tray.  And then there was Pepsi in her thick, fancy glasses on a hot summer day. The best thing I have ever tasted. All we ever really had at home was Kool-Aid and buttermilk.  Disgusting.  Once I was done with the yard or painting the garage or helping move the big flat rocks in a nice circle around her tree, she would go buy ice cream and chocolate syrup to make sundaes as a reward.  Grandma Rose lived down the road from Hogue's Super Market and I had a little sweet tooth just like her. Later in life, we would call that Diabetes.

Of course, there had to be a day when I got injured.  Grandma had a tool that I was allowed to use to cut down the tall, thick weeds on the side of the house. It looked like a rake on both sides, but it was metal and had teeth.  I would swing it back and forth and knock down the tall weeds.  I couldn't mow there because there were rocks where the weeds grew, so it just needed cut down.  Of course, one day I tripped over a rock while I was swinging the shin-killer and took a piece of my skin with it.  It sliced me up pretty good and immediately, blood streaked from the gash down my leg. Right on the shin.  I immediately put my dirty hands over it to keep it from pouring out, but my sock was already soaked, and blood was filling up in my shoe.  I took off my sock and held it over my gash. It was almost as long as my finger. I hobbled in to show Grandma.  She took me home to show my dad after we got the bloody scene cleaned up.  When I moved my second sock I was holding over the gash (because the first sock was soaked), blood pooled back up into the gash and spilled over.  He took one look at it and said it was going to heal up perfectly fine.  He got a kitchen towel and some ice and told me to put my leg up higher than my heart.

I felt woozy like I was going to puke but didn't. I sat in the living room by myself until the ice was all starting to melt, and the towel was wet and leaking. I got up to put the towel and ice in the sink.

My dad came and checked on my leg for an update. I was hoping this wasn't how I ended up with an amputated leg! He borrowed some butterfly stitches from the neighbors. He put about 4 of those across the gash and it held up pretty nicely except for the part where there was a missing chunk of skin. I told him I thought I needed stitches, but we didn't have any insurance or money for anything like that. When I went to bed that night, I used a small needle and some brown thread and gave myself a few stiches to pull the open part back together. My leg was on fire and burning with pain for about 2 days. Eventually it scabbed up and I used the toenail clippers to cut my "stitches" out about 2 weeks later. Later that summer one of the pieces of thread came oozing out of the gash that seemed to take months to heal. But by the end of summer, it was hardly a noticeable scar. And like always, I survived.

Life seemed to be moving along smooth, with Beth gone. We had electric the whole time. We had water. We had a phone. We had cable tv and a remote control. It seemed like we finally had some stability in the house and maybe from selling the marijuana, we had a little more money to spare. We didn't have fights in the house anymore. But, one day, I came home from school to a whole new problem. My dad was covered in blood, passed out on the couch and the cops were at my house. We came in the house from the back door and there were cops in the living room. We had no idea what was going on. Lanny was sitting on the front porch talking to one of the cops. Dad was not moving on the couch, and we could hear an ambulance coming. One of the officers wrapped dad's hand in a towel to stop the bleeding and dad's eyes opened. He raised his eyebrows a little but didn't say a word.

At least he wasn't dead. That was the first thing we thought of when we came into the house. The cops asked us to go sit on the porch with Lanny once they noticed we had come in the back door.

Lanny called grandma. Lanny also called the ambulance when he came home from school and found dad bleeding on the couch. But Beth called the cops and sent them to look for dad. Evidently, dad found Beth at another man's trailer. Beth, my dad, and her new man got into an altercation. Beth's new man stabbed my dad in the hand with a pair of scissors. So, my dad beat her to a bloody pulp with a snow shovel. At least that is the story we were told. It is quite possible he beat her with the shovel first and then was stabbed in the hand. Either way, she had a broken face, and my dad broke both of her arms at the elbow. She was never able to paint the same again.

We stayed a few nights with grandma until dad made bail. She probably paid for that and the attorney that handled his case. We went about our days like it was normal to come home to a house full of cops, a bloody parent, and blood all over the floor. Then out of the blue, my mother showed up for dinner. She was never really mentioned in the prior years and no one ever asked about her. I was scared of her at first because I didn't know her and hadn't seen her in over 3 years. She told us dad called her to come see us as he was in trouble. Dad called us all in the kitchen and asked us to just talk to her and enjoy our dinner. We all sat back down at the table staring at her and staring at our food. No one ate, and no one talked. I still felt I wanted something more in life and I felt like this woman, my mother, should have me and give me a better life. During that dinner, I followed her in the bathroom and begged her to take me with her, to please take me and be my mom, and love me and do my hair and help me with homework. I didn't care where she lived. I wanted a home. I wanted a mom who loved me. I wanted to be loved by my mother. I asked if I could be her daughter for real. I asked her a million questions. I asked her where she lived, if she had cable, if she had electric, if she had a job, if she wanted us. I asked her if she had a baby and where it is. I asked her if she knew my dog died and my teacher died. I asked her if she loved me. She told me she loved me. She has always loved me. She wiped my tears and told me not to cry. She was crying too and smearing black makeup down her face. She said she would always do what was best for me. She looked so beautiful, just as beautiful as I ever remembered. Mom was living in the state of Washington. She never answered all my questions. I just stared at her long, dark curly hair, makeup, lipstick, painted fingernails, and a white business suit. She smelled so pretty wearing lots of perfume. She spoke with an accent, and I thought that was cool. But otherwise, she was a stranger, and I didn't hardly remember her. But I just knew I wanted to go.

She never finished dinner with us. She left shortly after that bathroom trip and I thought she would be back to get me, maybe tonight, maybe tomorrow, maybe the next day or the next... So, I packed my bag. The only things I needed were, of course, my red jeans outfit and lavender sweater. I kept my bag ready and packed. A little red duffle bag with white handles under my bed. If I wore my sweater, I made sure to put it back in my bag just in case. But she never did come for me. I never stopped hoping one day she would come get me. Save me. Begging my mom to take me with her was one of the most compelling reminders of my desire to be taken care of. For the rest of my life, I remember feeling a huge betrayal to my father by asking her to take me, begging her to take me. But that was one moment of my life I had to live with that I would never regret and would never feel the need to apologize for. Afterall, I didn't get what I wanted. At 10, I still had everyone else making my life's decisions for me. I was hoping to find something better. I thought maybe there was a better place for me. I just wanted to find it. I felt so rejected and small. I felt so worthless that my own mother didn't even want me. There must have been something wrong with me. I was probably too ugly, or small, or dumb, or something. Thoughts of betrayal came over me as well because I betrayed the one parent who actually did want me, for nothing. I wrestled with this turmoil inside of me and it gave me a stomachache. If it were up to me, my next wish would have been to go back to the beach and live there by myself, away from everyone and just have peace. Me and the water. Me and the beach. Me and the fish. The last time I remember feeling truly happy. Where the sun shined on my face and tanned my skin. Where the marmalade sunsets were so beautiful, you forget about being hungry or sad or alone. I just wanted to go back. Before Mrs. Woodruff died. Before I lost the book. Before Sandy died. Before my dad was bloody on the couch. When I was happiest. I dreamed of being in a happy place and hoped for a happy home. But we don't always get what we want.

# CHAPTER SEVEN

# The Frost

Grandma Rose took us to court hearings for the trial from the beating of Beth, which took months before the hearing started and weeks for the actual trial. Dad was found guilty of Felonious Assault, of course, because he was. Seeing Beth in the courtroom made me feel sorry for her because she looked awful. I felt so sad for her not being able to paint. She still had lots of bandages on her arms, and you could tell she must have had to have surgery, as there were big scars on the top part and bottom part of her arms. She just looked tired. I wondered if she would want us because we didn't have anywhere else to go long term if dad had to go to jail. But of course, she didn't. She wouldn't even look at us. Of course, we belonged to this monster of a man who could have very easily ended her life. We were mean to her, and we were pretty sure she never liked us in the first place. That was ok because we never liked her either. She wasn't an affectionate person to us. No one ever was.

Once Dad was found guilty, we were called into a big meeting in the lawyer's office with Grandma Rose, who also probably paid for dad's attorney. The Judge asked if we wanted to go with our mom. After she disappeared after dinner months ago, I didn't think she was an option any longer. I didn't know what to say. I was scared and I was sick to my stomach, because I had already resigned myself that she didn't want me, or she would have taken me when I asked her to. My dad was going to be sent to prison and we needed to figure this out. Now. Literally like now, because he was taken away and locked up right when the hearing ended. Dad was going to be locked up until he was sentenced. The Judge asked us all again if we wanted to go with our mom. Christian was the first to answer and he said yes. Lanny said no. Lola and I just stared at each other for what seemed like an eternity asking each other with our eyes what the other one wanted to do. We both said no at the same time. Since the majority of us said no, it was decided we would go into foster care. We didn't know that saying no to our mom, meant foster care. My grandma Rose loved us and lived in a tiny little house on the corner of Kilbourne Street and Shumaker Drive. I assume she was not able or willing to take all 4 of us. With my dad going to prison, I don't think she would be able to handle or afford all of us for that entire time. Grandma only had one extra bedroom. Even if she could only take one, how could she just pick one?

Once we went into foster care, that was the first time I was separated from Lola. I think back to both of us saying no at the same time and wonder if that one word changed our trajectory in life forever. Would this be a better path? Would we have been better off going with our mother? I felt the weight of the world in the pit of my stomach thinking that one word separated us for what seemed like an eternity in little sister time. During childhood, she had always been my protector.

She was always a head and shoulders bigger than me. Only a year older but she always seemed so much more mature. I was almost 11 and still very shy, small, scrawny, skinny, and dependent on someone else. I felt fragile compared to my big sister. She had just turned 12. She was physically very mature and emotionally even more mature. She always looked over me whether I wanted her to or not. At that time, at her age and Lanny's age, they weren't suitable for a foster home. They were too old. They ended up in a receiving home in Norwalk, which is basically a juvenile detention center. I remember worrying that they were in a juvenile jail and were probably mis-treated. Of course, that was no place for either of them. They were exposed to kids who were there because they were drinking and doing drugs. My sister, already mature beyond her years, had no business being exposed in that type of environment and it sent her into a path of misbehavior that she would struggle with for years for come. She made friends and connected with some of the girls who were there who had criminal records, got into fist fights, and drank alcohol. She should have never been there.

Christian and I went together to a foster home in the same town we were living in. Great thing is, no school change. But the downside was, everyone knew what happened. And in Bellevue, EVERYONE talked about it. It was embarrassing, but I pretended not to pay attention. Afterall, I wasn't that important that people cared about my life or my dad. I was just a kid trying to get by and be left alone. And I just wanted to be left alone. I didn't want to talk to people, and I didn't want people talking to me. I was drained inside from feelings. I didn't really have anymore.

People can say what they want about foster care being awful, but I can say I enjoyed my foster home. We landed in a great foster home in the early 80's and it was a blessing to me and Christian. Our foster parents were licensed through Huron County Human Services. That department would make headlines many years later with a few horror stories coming from out of home care.  In 2004, a Huron County foster parent stabbed an 11-year-old foster child five times. Allegedly, he was protecting other members of his family from her.  She bled to death in their barn. The foster father was convicted of voluntary manslaughter and was sentenced to a three-year prison term. In the wrongful death suit, the Huron County officials testified that they had several child abuse complaints involving the foster father including sexual, physical, and emotional abuse allegations.  But none of that deterred them from licensing him as a foster parent. Several years later in 2007, the family was awarded $600,000 in the wrongful death suit. That money likely ended up in the hands of the child's father who was an alleged heroin-addict, and her mother whose heroin positive newborn prompted the 11-year-old and other siblings ending up in foster care.

Another Huron County black eye came on the heels of a notorious story that became known nationally as the "caged kids" case.  There were 11 adopted children living in an environment not suitable for animals.  The 11 victims from this case reached a two-million-dollar settlement in 2014 from Ohio's Stark County, where three of them lived before being placed with their awful adoptive parents who forced them to sleep in cages. They reached a 1.2-million-dollar settlement with Huron County where some of the others resided before being placed with their adoptive parents in Wakeman in north central Ohio. The professionals overseeing their placement and care were also berated for their role of the suffering of these children.  When they were rescued in 2005, they ranged in age from 1 to 14. Some of the older children used the money to pay for college.  Some of the children had been alleged to be of such severe behavioral or special needs that the family tried to use that as a justification of their unusual sleeping arrangements. However, as time drew out more information, it appeared at the family wrongly portrayed the children as troubled for their own gain. The cages were homemade and made of wire and wood. The children were also abused including allegations like shoving their heads in toilets and flushing it, beating them with sticks and boards, and hosing them off outside of the house in the winter.

With horror stories like these making headlines across the country, it is frightening to think about the thousands of children in foster care at the mercy of the proper screening of adults in charge of caring for our most vulnerable population. But those cases are anomalies. For the most part, foster parents are the most giving and beautiful people who exist in this world. They share their homes with children in crisis who are traumatized. They open their homes and their hearts for these temporary guests. What an amazing gift they are to the child welfare field!

I was lucky I was with a family and not in the receiving home. According to myself as my only fan of myself, I was also smart and easy-going, but I am sure adults would describe me a little differently. I'm sure they thought I was shy and quiet and weird. I don't know why, but during this time I also started to feel ugly. Compared to my mom and my sister, I felt inferior in appearance. I felt plain and overall, just ugly. But I did start to realize at this age, that I was going to need to be smart and stay smart, especially because I felt ugly. I became more and more interested in school, and reading the dictionary was my favorite past-time. I would highlight words I liked, like diarrhea and flippant. I always dreamed I would study this book and one day, I would win a spelling-bee or use funny words when I write a book one day. Yeah, I was a total weirdo. I didn't have many friends. I didn't trust many people and I didn't like everyone else. I just wanted to blend into the wall, so no one looked at me or talked to me.

My foster home was warm.  There was a big register grate in the middle of the living room floor.  We were allowed to sit there and eat breakfast.  I put my new fuzzy slippers on the grates and the warmth would melt lines in the bottoms.  They were my first ever pair of slippers. They were blue with white snowflakes on the outside with fuzzy, white fur inside.  My foster parents: Dodie and Alfred, were good parents to their kids.  They had a piano and Dodie would teach me music.  I learned how to read music notes and where they corresponded on the piano.  Dodie and Al had two girls and a boy.  I was a little older than the girls and Christian was the same age as their son.  The girls had one room in the A-frame house and the boys had another.  The ceilings were slanted, and I had my very own dresser to put my clothes in.  I never had a dresser.  But it didn't matter because I didn't have any clothes to put in there.

Dodie made sure we ate breakfast every morning.  EVERY morning we had breakfast.  This was so weird.  Their kids got to choose if they wanted milk in their cereal, not just because there wasn't any milk.  Dodie was a nurse, and she was a hugger and a talker.  Alfred liked football and I liked Alfred.  He would let me sit with him when he watched a football game and he didn't get drunk or drink beer, which was also so weird.  His favorite team was the same as my dad's favorite team and I loved it! It was nice to have something that reminded me of home. Christian kept to himself, and I began ignoring him.  I didn't want to people to think I was annoying too. We became a part of their family while we were there. We went to the doctor and dentist for the first time I could ever remember.  The dentist was pleased with my teeth.  We were behind on shots, but otherwise, we checked out ok, I think.  We got some new clothes, not just a new outfit.  Actual new clothes. And I got moon boots for winter just like everyone else would wear.  I was so excited to show my boots to my teacher.

We spent time with Dodie and Alfred and their extended family. We would also go to Alfred's brother's house and other relatives' houses for meals and holidays and family games. They would spend time together a lot, and they had other kids to play games with and watch movies. It was nice to learn about family visits and just hanging out with each other because they wanted to, and it sometimes had nothing to do with a holiday or event. They were huggers too. I especially liked the food, the meals, and the cooking. I liked to hang out with Dodie's dad. He was old and funny and farted a lot. I knew a thing or two about this. During our stay in foster care, Dodie's dad became sick. He was in the hospital and had cancer in his brain. He wasn't doing well. I remember asking to go with Dodie to see him in the hospital. She cried and I felt weird feeling sad for her and sad for him, for these strangers that didn't know me, but I cared about her being sad. She, of course hugged me and I think this was the first time I felt like hugging someone back. And not long after he got sick, he died.

There was family stuff and meals and crying, and mainly I just wanted to get out of this house and go back to my house where people didn't care, and people didn't cry! I liked this place better when it was holidays and football and food and farting. I always wanted to go back in time. Away from the sadness. I don't like it. I wanted to go back to that time in the bathroom and tell my mom to just fuck off and fuck you. I wanted to take back asking her to take me so she couldn't fuck me over. I wanted to go back to that lawyer's office and tell them they could send us to foster care but not take away my sister. I wanted to tell everyone to fuck off. I wanted to blame everyone for life sucking. I didn't know God or feel very much faith or hope in my life. But at this point, I felt so alone and even God himself was useless. My sister was gone. My dad was gone. Lanny was gone. Andrew was gone. My dog was gone. I don't like the feeling in my throat that makes me feel like sadness is trying to choke me. I hated my life.  I hated myself. I felt so lost. Trying to understand the death of a parent that Dodie was feeling, felt a lot like they just disappeared, and you don't see them again or talk to them again.  It felt a lot like my mom. I felt like she died too. And when Dodie was sad, I got sad remembering everything that died in my life.  Dodie wanted to call her dad and tell him about her day, and then she would cry because she couldn't.  I told her I knew what that felt like. I told her I don't have a phone number for my mom or even know where she lives or if she even knows where I am.  Dodie was a great mom, and she was a good listener when she wasn't talking.  I didn't talk a lot about how I felt, but she always found a way to figure those things out. She was a hard-working, strong lady. She didn't miss much work.  She cooked and cleaned and never seemed to stop doing all the mom stuff. I thought she was amazing. Dodie would never leave her kid in the bathroom. Dodie would never go years not seeing her kids. Dodie would lay down in front of a train for her kids, and she made sure they knew it. Dodie was a real mom. Dodie said she knew just what I needed.  Dodie said she would make sure I get to see my dad. This woman in her own grief was still trying to find ways to help me.  What an amazing human being.

True to her word, Dodie came to wake me up one weekend to tell me I was going on a visit. Grandma Rose came to pick me up and took me with her on a drive to see my dad in prison. I only went once. I was shaking so bad from nerves that my teeth started chattering. I couldn't control my legs shaking and I was scared to death.  I had butterflies in my stomach, and gas pains so bad because I was afraid to ask to go to the bathroom.  I'm sure the search to let us into prison was relaxed by today's standards, but I was wide-eyed and dry-mouthed.  I was afraid that I was going to get locked in and not be allowed to leave.  The visit was short and sweet and made me feel a whole lot better knowing that my dad was alive, and that he didn't disappear like my mom did. I felt better knowing where he was, even if it was in prison. I needed that little glimmer of hope and feeling of home that only came from my dad. I needed to hold on to the things that I did still have and remember not everything was gone in my life. I got to see he was ok and not have to wonder what it was like in the big house. He cried when he got to see me, his little "Nanny". He was allowed to give me one hug and I thought my whole life felt so much better for one second. I cried and tears dripped on his prison shirt. The guard gave me a Kleenex to blow my nose. And this is why I don't like to cry. It's like the tears and snot both come out at the same time, and it is annoying. And gross.

Dad gave me a bunch of drawings that his cell mate drew of us kids. They were colored pencil drawings of our school pictures dad said he had hanging on his wall. They looked just like our pictures. Dad was excited to tell us he was allowed to work on a farm at the prison in Chillicothe. And the best news of all, he was being prepared to get out! I have no idea how long he was sentenced to prison. But back in those days, they had shock parole. If he served 6 successful months of prison time, he could be let out on good behavior in that short period of time. I have no doubt he should have been sentenced to years in prison, and to be let out after 6 short months was actually shocking. Maybe that is why they called it shock parole. But this was the best news I had in a long time. I could feel the sense of hope and excitement coming back in my heart, what little was left of it.

My Grandma Rose and a lady friend of hers, Carmine, got us a duplex house just outside of Bellevue on Route 20. They set up the home and got all of us kids for visits. We put up beds and cleaned and painted to make the house our own. I loved staying with my foster family, but visiting here with Lanny and Lola was better than butter pecan ice cream. We eventually began staying in the duplex to prepare things for my dad to come home. I said goodbye to Dodie and Alfred. She was one of the most influential pieces of my childhood that really reminded me that there were different ways to live, different ways to parent, and better ways to take care of children. This time with Dodie and Al stayed with me forever and I am so grateful to have had some semblance of what a normal family should look like.

Grandma Rose and Carmine would take turns staying with us, and we were all 4 back together again. It seemed like years, but we were only in foster care for 6 months. But being away from Lola was not good. She came back angry at the world, and no one could blame her. She came back and seemed to have aged 5 years and seemed to just take on the world and everyone else like she owned the place. I still felt like a shy, little kid who still needed a parent. Carmine was a decent lady, but she was in love with my dad. She had known him for years and was a good friend of grandma's. I think she was trying to set him up with a good woman who didn't drink and party. We were sure, she wasn't dad's type! She was a bit of a bigger woman and had really thin, fluffy blonde hair. She also had a few fake teeth. She was nice and all, but by her looks alone, we knew she wouldn't be around long. My mom and Beth, I would at least say were thin and good-looking. All we could do was hope for the best.

We finally got to stay in our home with Carmine the night before dad got home. She made us all spaghetti and it was disgusting. I tried not to be rude and not eat, but I didn't really like it at all. Not long after eating, I tried to run downstairs to make it to the bathroom to puke and didn't quite make it. I puked all over the stairs. Nasty noodles all over. Carmine was a little grossed out and made it a point to let me know she had no intentions of cleaning up my mess. She gave me a bucket of warm water and a cloth and told me to clean my puke up off the steps. That sucked. I assure you; this was another one of those pukes I had no intentions of eating. I don't know what she put in the sauce, but it immediately turned my stomach.

Grandma Rose helped dad furnish the house. We finished up 6th grade here and had a wonderful summer with dad coming home. We were allowed to get another dog, although we could barely take care of ourselves without grandma's help. We got a Black Chow for free. Someone dad was working for had puppies and we got one. She was beautiful and fluffy, and we named her Bear. Dad was on parole and dad was on his best behavior initially. We think he got shock parole so he could come home and take care of his 4 kids, but I really don't know how that worked back in those days. Carmine was quickly kicked to the curb, and we didn't see her much after dad got out. We spent a lot of time growing a garden, having bon fires and running around the yard with Bear. We had a barn behind the house, and we would play in there where there were also some barn kittens. We would go fishing a lot, and just loved to ride around in dad's truck. That summer we seemed to spend every day outside, and just soaked each other up as a family.

We started up the next school year and I had to ride the bus to school in 7th grade. I began to make a few friends, although I was quite embarrassed of my home life. My friends came from good homes, and I was allowed to stay the night with them. I was introduced to great parents and learned how to dress and do my hair from my friends. A few of us were invited to stay over at Victoria's house. She was in my elementary school for 5th and 6th grade. She lived next to Aunt Gail in the same home where we were rescued after the blizzard of '78. My cousin Steven and Victoria's older brother were really good friends when they were neighbors. Victoria had a September birthday and made a new friend from one of the other elementary schools, Stacy. Over the summer they played on a softball team together. They had a little get together for both of their birthdays and invited a bunch of the girls over to Victoria's house. I also got to spend the night once at Jill's house. She invited a group of us over to spend the night. All the girls had been there before, but I had not. When I got dropped off, I was a little overwhelmed at how big this house was. I couldn't find my way around and the girls took off and hid from me. I wandered around for what seemed like an hour not knowing if I would ever find Jill's bedroom. She had an indoor pool, a walk-in refrigerator, a beautiful staircase in the front of the house, another back set of stairs and an elevator. I was literally lost. And I even had a chance to have a few of them spend the night at our country house on Route 20. We had a fun time playing loud music, running around the yard, and watching a scary movie on the TV with pizza and popcorn. My dad was always a gracious host and has the funniest personality. All of my friends just loved him.

My dad still never worked steady, and we always teetered on financial crisis. At this home, we had bedrooms. We had plenty of room to run and we were happy. We had a microwave for the first time, cable tv, and burritos! We were together, all of us. I had all my outfits from Dodie's house, my snow boots still fit, a few new outfits from Carmine and my favorite purple swishy pants. Grandma Rose helped a lot. She bought me purple leotards and tights for gymnastics. She paid for gymnastics. Victoria was in my gymnastics class. She bought me new sweaters. And she would pick us up and drive us to McDonald's for fish sandwiches, fries and milkshakes almost every Sunday. She would also stop the car and threaten to beat our asses because we liked to hum to the music, and it would drive her nuts. So, we did that a lot. Those drives to Clyde with my Grandma were the best weekends.

She also drove a Lincoln Continental and I felt like I was royalty being chauffeured around by her. One of her most recent husbands bought the car for her. I think that would have been husband #5 at that point. Grandma was a "serial marryer." I know that's not a word, but I don't know how else to say it. I don't know how she managed to find so many husbands, but she was always married.

I also made the basketball team with my friends. Our team was really good. Victoria and Stacy were really good. They had been playing together for a while. But I didn't play a lot. I just loved to be on the team and made friends with the other girls. They all had braces. But I was lucky, my teeth were perfectly straight without them. Because lord knows, if they weren't straight, there was no way we could ever afford braces. I also joined the track team and made even more friends. I still loved to run. And I also added hurdles to the running. Track was fun. I didn't have a care in the world when I was running. And I still made sure to get straight A's.

At the country house, we loved playing outside and getting dirty. Bear had puppies, and we were allowed to keep one. We picked the one with the pointiest ears and named him Gizmo. We were obsessed with the Gremlins movie when it came out and we had a TV to watch it on! We also watched football on Sundays. I think this is the main reason we never went to church, besides the fact my dad didn't belong to a church and didn't follow anyone's rules, or the law, so it made sense we never, ever went. My dad made meals out of whatever we had in the house, and it was always good. We loved hobo stew, which was never the same. Sometimes it was broth and corn and green beans and beef stew bites. And other times it was potatoes and carrots and cabbage and ham and whatever else we had to throw in there.

We grew huge gardens and I learned how to pick beans and shuck corn. We loved the drive-in for movies. It was the only way we could take a truck load of kids and get in for cheap.  I was even allowed to invite my friends. We loved scary movies and popcorn and seemed like we would be making a good life out here in the country house.  But life for us was like walking across a frozen pond.  You got to wonder when or where it might crack, and you fall in.  We rallied around the television for some hobo stew and football.  One Sunday, our team's beloved quarterback, Joe Theismann, got his leg snapped during a game.  We watched the replay over and over and were stunned.  We lost our quarterback.  And eventually, life's tornado came rolling back in to shake up our world even worse than Joe's broken leg bones.

Dad went from working every day and being home every night to working less. We had less food. And he would leave at night staying out later and later. He stayed out late, more and more.  And our settled life, began to unsettle.  We spent more time at home and were alone more and more also.  We spent time playing the quiet game.  No laughing. No talking.  If we made noise, Lanny would twist up a small towel and flick us with it. He only had one shot, so if he missed, he missed.  The worst ones were when the end of the towel was wet.  That hurt like hell.  We were way better at cooking and having a microwave made it easier for us.

One day, out of the blue, dad shows up to introduce us to his new "girlfriend."  Not only was she young, but she was trashy.  I mean, TRAAAASHY.  We stared at her. She had on tight bell-bottom jeans and a half shirt. She had long, black, stringy hair parted in the middle that hung down her back like Cher, except this bitch was uglier. And she had on hideous red lipstick and moccasins.  Instant dislike. She smoked and smelled like stale cigarette smoke on her clothes and breath. We all thought she was disgusting. Yet, she looked very familiar. We had met her once before.  She had babysat for us when we stayed for a short time in the trailer park in Castalia right when we first moved back to Ohio.  In addition to being gross, she was dumb. I didn't have the patience for a dumb adult in my life. She tried to talk to us and make conversation, but we were just flabbergasted trying to understand how this "woman" could think she could come in this house and try to "mother" us.  We didn't need a mother.  Our real mom didn't want us, and we didn't want a fake one.

And the biggest problem of all, she had 4 KIDS. SHE HAD 4 KIDS! Oh, my fucking God have mercy, let's just add chaos to chaos and hope for the best. Not only had we met her once before, but our mom also met her way back. Her name was Ellen.  The same Ellen mom worked with at the trucker diner all those years ago whose husband would flirt with mom. If this was life's way of giving us a full circle moment, I would like life to take the fucking circle back and shove it up its ass. And take those 4 kids with it.

# CHAPTER EIGHT

# The Tsunami

Without sugar coating anything, as I never was able to do such a thing; Ellen was a terrible human being and an even worse mom. And thankfully I had a little bit of an idea of what a mom was supposed to be like. Dodie was a good mom. Ellen couldn't hold a candle to Dodie. She probably couldn't even spell candle. I almost survived the entire first year of junior high without a catastrophe landing right on my life. Why would I think anything could just be smooth sailing and life could be good? We became instant babysitters. We instantly became a group of US and THEM. THEM consisted of her 4 kids, HER, and my dad. He became one of them and we kicked him out of the US. We were pretty sure this was a disaster waiting to happen and none of US wanted anything to do with any of THEM! At this point in life, Christian was 10, I was 12, Lola was 13, and Lanny was 16. US! THEM consisted of Karley, 9; Lee, 7; Brian, 3; and Bailey, 1. 8 fucking kids! Jesus Christ in tube socks, what the fuck.

Bailey was in diapers and that was a deal breaker. He didn't know any better. He couldn't talk, which made him tolerable. Brian would cry when his mom left the home, forever it seemed like. He was always sick, always sniffing and sucking his boogers. He was disgusting. Lee usually kept to himself and didn't say much. Karley was annoying from the first minute. At 9, as a girl, with all these little brothers, we expected her to mother them more and take care of them, like we did with each other. But she didn't. She was lazy. So, there were constant fights of US telling HER to take care of her brothers, change diapers, clean up after them, etc. She usually didn't, which is no surprise she didn't know how to mother her siblings. She had a terrible mother as an example to learn from. We didn't know much about what a mom is supposed to do, but we were pretty sure, Ellen was a far cry from being a good mom. Her kids wore dirty clothes. We didn't understand that even though we were poor also, we were never dirty. Dad was never dirty. Ellen smelled like a musty car mat. There was nothing remotely attractive about her. She had nice hair, and she still had a nice body after 4 kids. I get it, that's what dad saw. But how could he not see all the kids as a fucking problem he didn't need to take on because he had 4 of his own to manage. Wasn't that enough?

I buried myself in homework, sports activities, practices, going to friends' houses, and even signed up to do a school play just to get out of the house and away from the chaos as much as I could. Being at home was no longer a salvation for me. My home became a fucking zoo with some dirty ass kids. Ellen chain-smoked. I could not stand the smell of cigarette smoke. I could not stand the smell of Ellen. I could not stand Ellen. Ellen also liked to drink. For someone who didn't have much money to take care of her own kids, she never went without her Coors Light and her cartons of cigarettes. She was also a firm believer in aliens. She would go on and on about alien stories and abduction and people she knew or stories she read about aliens. I just looked at her and asked her if she graduated high school. She said, "No. What does that have to do with anything?" I said "Exactly." I just could not understand how someone could believe in something you never saw with your own eyes. Which also makes me wonder, why do people say that? I "saw it with my own eyes." Like who else's eyes would you be seeing it with? Anyway, I felt this way about aliens, God, and Jesus. If you didn't see it, how do you know it is real? Why do you believe? What is missing in a person's brain that would make them believe something in their heart and soul is real, that they never saw themselves? I struggled with understanding this concept and felt this made her inferior to me since I felt so much smarter than her. She didn't like me condescending her and made sure to point out that she knows I think I am smarter than her. In my head I am saying, "Yes, yes I am smarter than you. My asshole is smarter than you, lady!"

Dad would take us to babysit these kids at their uncle's house and he would go out and play music and Ellen would follow along. Ellen was living with her sister's ex-husband down the road on Route 20 closer to town. This house was dirty. The kids were dirty. They smelled. The house smelled. The carpet was sticky. The kids were sticky. We were completely grossed out. Their repulsive mother, Ellen, didn't work. She liked to drink, play bingo and smoke cigarettes. Then she would play bingo, smoke cigarettes, and drink. The youngest boys had pop and Kool-Aid in their baby bottles. They had eternal Kool-Aid stains down the fronts of their bellies. I liked to shake Bailey's bottle and hold my finger on the nipple with pop in it until the nipple swelled so big like a balloon, I thought it would pop. Ellen just moved back to Ohio from Alabama. She was divorcing from the children's father due to him beating her ass, so she chose to pick a winner in my father! The father to all these kids was the same young cook at the diner where my mom worked who used to flirt with her, Lee, Sr. Ellen was just so ugly on the inside and had no idea how to make her outside be less ugly. She was tacky and was mean to her kids. Awful.

We spent the summer going back and forth with Ellen and I spent the summer going anywhere I could to get away from the house and these kids. I tried out and made the same softball team with Victoria and Stacy. Angela also played and she was our smart-mouthed catcher. She was really good at trash talking while the other team was up to bat. Victoria was our pitcher and she and Stacy had been playing for years, so they were really good at crushing the ball. Stacy played short stop and she was the most athletic of us all. I was starting to grow a little but had no muscle what-so-ever on my body. I was still just smaller than everyone else. I played in the outfield and was a little scared of the ball. I caught it when I had to, but I really liked batting. I was still pretty fast, so once I was on base, all I wanted to do was steal. I bunted a lot and got walked a lot, which also meant I was on base a lot and I scored a lot. Not far into the season, I became the lead-off hitter. Dad never went to any of my track meets or basketball games, and he never came to any of my softball games. I didn't care. We had so much fun. We played tournaments all over. In one tournament in Maumee, we were tied going to the bottom of the last inning. I got up to bat and was walked to start us off. We had two outs, but by that time I had stolen my way around to third base. Victoria was up to bat. She made a nice hit out into right field and scored me home, and we won that game and won the whole tournament. We had a blast that summer. The distraction was nice away from home, where life was getting messier and messier.

Ellen drove a muscle car, a Chevelle. She also liked to flex her muscles and show off arms, where she also had a tattoo of 5 cards, a Royal Flush. She loved John Cougar Mellencamp and dancing like a whore. She really spent her life like she didn't have kids and it was disgusting to watch her come and go as she pleased. Dad and Ellen decided to combine households. Starting in 8th grade, our lives were combined with theirs and I still did everything I could in school and sports and with friends to get out of the house. I studied and did homework and concentrated on my grades to make sure I never fell behind. I did my work over and over and wrote notes and stayed busy so that I wasn't bothered by anyone when asked to help with the kids. I would always say I was doing homework when in actuality, I was just copying my history book word for word onto paper. The good thing about that was not only did I read it, but I committed it to memory by copying the words. I could remember where each chapter started and where words and definitions were on the page. I was able to train myself to remember what I was copying in a photographic way, while at the same time committing it to memory. We had a trial in our history class and had to create what a hearing would look like in our classroom. I was profoundly interested in learning about the pieces of a trial. As a child living through my father's trial, I didn't understand the different roles of the two attorneys, Prosecutor and Defense. And I certainly didn't understand the role of the Judge. This trial in class was so intriguing to me that I thought maybe someday I could be a lawyer. And I sat that thought in the back of my mind for a while. I didn't have a class I didn't love or excel in. I even liked our home economics class and learning to sew. I made a little stuffed elephant for my sewing project and an apron. I still enjoyed everything about school. I have always enjoyed every teacher.

In Science class with Mr. Marvin, I loved learning about the periodic table and the elements. I took as many notes as I could and was really excited when he wheeled a tv into our classroom to watch a U.S. space shuttle launch from Cape Canaveral, Florida live. Everyone was most excited about a teacher, Christa McAuliffe, a civilian, being part of the crew of the Challenger and the first civilian in space. On January 28, 1986, our 7th grade science class watched the take off with such excitement. In less than 2 minutes, the excitement of the class turned to horror when the Challenger exploded right before us and the space shuttle and the trail of smoke behind it turned into an exploding cloud that trailed off. Mr. Marvin quickly turned the tv off and assured the class, we will have to come back to that and see what the update is later. But we all knew. Everyone who was watching knew that everyone on that space shuttle just died in that explosion, including Christa McAuliffe. The little red-headed, freckle-faced boy with braces sitting beside me was crying. I looked around the room and several class members were crying. We could hear lots of noise in the hallway as everyone opened up their doors to talk to the teachers across the hallway. No one spoke until it was time to go to the next class. Of course, everyone talked about it throughout the school day, and even President Ronald Reagan came on the tv later to express sincere condolences to the families of those on board. It was terrifying.

The best part about 7th grade was having my sister in the same school as me in 8th grade. If anyone thought about picking on me because I was still a little, skinny ugly bird, she would make them think twice. And they did. No one bothered me, and boys paid a lot of attention to my friends, but I was usually just the weird, awkward friend that tagged along everywhere. At the end of the school year, there was a talent competition. Lola sang one of our favorite songs, "Country Roads" by John Denver. The kids in this school didn't really appreciate country music as much as we did as we grew up on it and loved it. She was a good singer, but she acted like she was shy and didn't do a good job. I loved it!

We left the country house and moved to the other side of town over the summer going into the 8<sup>th</sup> grade.  We would move around several different homes in Bellevue due to not paying rent and destroying the houses.  We left our country home and stayed for a short time with Ellen in a duplex she rented down the road from her mother.  It was new and nice when we first started staying there on the corner of Sinclair Street and Route 20.  We were only there for a few months before we found a bigger house for us all. Ellen was not a housekeeper and did not clean up after her kids.  And they did not clean up after themselves. Lanny, Lola and I stayed in the new house by ourselves for a while until Ellen was able to get her shit packed from her dirty dump and move her and her rug rats in. She was also pregnant but that didn't stop her from continuing to drink and smoke.  And it also didn't stop her from thinking she can roller skate while she is pregnant.  She ended up tripping and falling and breaking her leg.  She ended up in a cast with crutches and that really slowed down what very little attention she gave to her children.  Now they had to help her.  It was pathetic. Lanny was going to be a senior in high school, and he had drinking parties. Lola was 14 and I was 13.  There was still such a huge maturity gap between us that people thought she was my mom.  She had boobs and hips and looked like a woman. She was tall and tan with long dark hair and she was dating a boy who was entering the military.  My dad struggled with Lola's independence and being so grown up beyond her years, that there was no way ignorant Ellen was going to come in here and try to tell her what to do.  I was referred to as a "carpenter's dream, flat as a board".  I was still actively involved in sports and Lanny was playing football for the local high school.  He was still a very good football player, and his girlfriend, Renee was a cheerleader.  She was adorable and sweet and just the kind of person our family needed to make sure we weren't surrounded by total failures.

And that summer I was partying with alcohol and marijuana. I was having a ball because I had no mother, and for this summer, I had no father either. At one point during the summer, Lola was sent off to stay with an aunt in West Virginia. I'm not sure who made this happen, her or dad, but while she was home, she was getting into a lot of trouble. The relationship with Ellen was not getting off to a good start. Lola told this bitch on more than one occasion where she should shove her attitude. Lola stole the car a few times. Lola had the cops called on her several times. She and Ellen got physical with each other, but I was afraid to stick up for myself. No way was I interested in getting hurt. But Lola was taking a path of her own, and I was still trying to blend into the wall and not be noticed by anyone.

One morning after one of Lanny's all-night parties, Lola continued to puke off and on throughout the day. Dad hadn't moved his skanky woman fully into the house yet, so he stopped over later in the day to check on us and Lola was still puking. For a long time, we thought it must be a super shitty hangover, but after more and more hours of her not getting better and seeming to get weaker and weaker, my dad had to take her to the emergency room. Turns out, she had a ruptured appendix and was dangerously ill due to it. If she hadn't gotten to the hospital when she did, she seriously could have died. She had an emergency surgery to remove her appendix. I don't even want to know how or if that was ever paid for. Up until then, we rarely saw a doctor for anything. When I needed a physical signed for sports, my dad would sign and date it and turn it in. We didn't have any insurance. And I am pretty sure we didn't have shots either, he just filled out that form too with whatever dates just to make it work and no one said anything.

My dad always worked under the table and never filed income tax returns. Although with 8 kids in the house, he probably wouldn't have anything to worry about for taxes. There was a show back in the day called "8 is enough" and it literally is more than enough. But apparently dad and Ellen didn't seem to agree with that. In September of 1986, at the start of my 8th grade year when we were all living in the same house, little Joey was born into the family. I was shocked to see he came out looking normal although he was a little small, probably due to the smoking and drinking. I didn't really know much about her pregnancy as I talked to her as little as possible and didn't really care. Some of us went to the hospital to meet little Joey and even though I got to see him, I was not thrilled that we had another baby in the house. He was super cute and favored my dad quite a bit.

We had just gotten Bailey out of diapers, and then along came Joey. All I could think about was this part in my Judy Blume book, Tales of a Fourth Grade Nothing: "I thought how great it would be if we could trade in Fudge for a nice cocker spaniel." Even with our bad track record with dogs, I would rather have a dog than Joey. One more kid we couldn't feed or clothe, and he never even had a crib. In school, I excelled in classes. I enjoyed studying and getting good grades. At this point, I was obsessed with making sure I got all A's. I also really focused on Art classes and enjoyed painting too. I got excellent grades in Art class and loved to draw. I also made a few more friends on my sports teams. In 7th and 8th grade, Lola had lots of boyfriends and was emotionally quite a bit more mature than I was. If anything, I was probably a bit immature for my age, and naïve. I was also still very skinny and quite frankly a bit of an ugly duckling. I knew it and so did everyone else. I hated my freckles, and I hated my curly, frizzy hair. It seemed no matter what I did, it was always a bit of a fuzzy mess. I kept my hair in a ponytail as often as I could.

Lola not only got in trouble at home fighting with the step-monster, but she would also get in fights at school. She was not shy with saying what she wanted. This school year, she was in high school, and I was at the junior high.  She took off with Ellen's car and got caught, a few times.  One night, at the high school football game, Lanny was playing a heck of a game. His name was announced a lot on the speaker.  He played free safety, and he was fast and could jump high for being a shorter guy. As the legend goes (just ask him, he will tell you), at 5'9" tall, he could dunk a volleyball. I didn't see it with my own eyes or anyone else's eyes so I can't swear to it, but he still makes this claim to this very day. However, during this game, he intercepted the ball in the end zone and ran it back for a touchdown which was a school record for the longest interception return for a touchdown. This is the kind of record that can never be broken because it is as long as it could possibly be in the stat books.  99-yard return.  But as life always is for this family, the good can't just linger without the cloud of darkness popping in to say hello.  During this game, the ambulance was called to the stands. The paramedics helped a youth attending the game onto a stretcher and to the ambulance for a short ride around the corner to the hospital, where my brother had died years back.  Once word got around that it was Lola in the stands, I found dad and we headed to the hospital.  We were met there with a group of kids from the game who were interested in seeing how she was doing, including her little middle school boyfriend, who was a popular boy from my grade. Turns out Lola was not only continuing to dabble with the alcohol, but she took a bunch of pills and was deemed suicidal. She was admitted to the hospital for a few days and released to home expected to get some follow up services that never took place.  Along with the hospital bill, going to therapy was also never going to be paid for.

The kids were terrors in school and at home.  They were like little destroyers, tearing up everything in their path.  The boys would be confined to one room. When Ellen would get tired of them, she would lock the door and lock them in there for hours.  They would piss in the corners of the closets because she wouldn't let them out to use the bathroom and were treated like animals.  Ellen wouldn't take care of anyone but herself.  One day after a basketball game, I came home to find the house was messier than normal.  The boys were bouncing all over, just into everything. Dad wasn't home for some reason, and normally these kids don't act this wild when he was around.  I was in the kitchen trying to pour a glass of Kool-Aid and see if we had any food to eat.  There was a sub from Subway in the bottom drawer, so I got that out and started to open it.  Ellen came into the kitchen to ask me what I was doing.  I told her I was looking for something to eat and found a sub.  She said it was her sub and it had her name on it and she snatched it out of my hands and wrapped it back up.  And sure as shit, it had her fucking name written on it in marker and it also said, "Do not eat."  She put it back in the fridge and slammed it shut. I opened the fridge back up again to put the Kool-Aid jug back in the fridge and Ellen shoved the door shut again. I dropped the jug and spilled it all out on the floor.  Ellen got pissed off and pushed me all the way against the wall with her hand on my throat.  She was in my face telling me, "You aren't better than everyone, princess.  You need to understand that, you piece of shit."  Lola came around the corner and immediately ran up and pushed Ellen away from me.  She said, "Don't you ever put your dirty fucking fingers on my sister, bitch!" Ellen and Lola started getting into a loud and heated argument.  My eyes just welled up into tears and I grabbed paper towels and started trying to soak up the Kool-Aid just as Dad walked in.  He also started yelling and Lola took off out the door. When he asked, "What the fuck is going on?"  I told him to "Ask his prized wife" and went upstairs to my room I was supposed to share with Lola and Karley, but Lola never came back home that night.

Ellen liked to pick at me and pick on me. She would always make comments calling me a princess or that I acted like I was better than her or her kids. I simply had no argument with her line of thinking and reasoning. I hated myself and hated my life, so if anyone thinks that my life or that I am better than her or her kids, then that makes her pretty low. She never made dinner regularly. She had one meal she knew how to cook, lasagna. She didn't clean up after herself or her kids. She never did laundry. She beat her kids with anything she could get her hands on. She locked the boys in rooms. I really don't remember anyone taking care of Joey. He was always just laying somewhere, and Karley was being yelled at by Ellen to get him a bottle, change his diaper, and to pick him up when he cried. He never had a baby bed or a crib or a playpen. I had no bond to Joey; I never even held him as a baby or tried to take care of him. I stayed away as much as I could. I hated being home. She treated all her kids like horrible shit. I didn't compare myself to them. They were reliant on her to meet all their needs and I didn't need her. I felt sorry for them. They weren't going to have a chance in hell at life with her as a mother. She is a disgusting human being. And a terrible example of a mother. I didn't even have one and it didn't take me long to figure that out.

Bellevue had a summer festival that lasted all weekend long. We looked forward to it every year. The best part of the Cherry Festival was the Cherry Festival Queen, and little Miss Cherry contests. Some of the outfits were so cute and as a young girl it was like our very own Ms. America contest. The girls were always so beautiful, and we always talked about which ones were our favorites. Of course, there was also a cherry pie baking contest. But it was also fun to ride rides and check out the boys. The rides were set up in the area around the Bellevue Recreation Center. We had so much fun, and the entire town loved the festival. Angela and I decided we were going to rip up some jeans and bleach them. We thought they looked so awesome when we showed up with our bleached ripped jeans. But some of the other kids asked us if we were in the pond because there must be piranhas in there. We didn't care. We felt like we made a pretty cool fashion statement, even though everyone was making fun of us.

The 8th grade school year seemed to fly by without any major issues. I still was friends with Victoria and Stacy and made a new friend who would come over and walk to football games with me sometimes, Jane. One of those days, she came into the house to do our hair a little bit before we walked to the school, and she noticed the door to the back of the house was locked. I told her to unlock it. No one was home and it shouldn't be locked anyway. However, all the boys were locked in the room and Ellen was gone. She even left the baby with the boys. They stunk and the room smelled horrible like pee when it opened. I asked them where dad or Karley and Ellen were and Lee said he had no idea, but they haven't been gone long. Joey was crying and Lee didn't know how to change his diaper, so I changed him and got him a bottle. I asked them if they wanted anything to eat or drink, and they all came out like concentration camp prisoners and scarfed down some snacks and Kool-Aid. They were just in their underwear and looked like someone had just cut all their hair down into buzz cuts. Jane was horrified. I just shook my head and told her Ellen does this to them all the time. They were in the front living room watching tv when Ellen and Karley came home. She immediately started yelling at them asking, "What the fuck are you doing out of your room?" I told her I let them out and if she locks them in there again, I am going to call the fucking cops on her. She initially started to go after me when she noticed my friend Jane standing there. She started to back peddle saying that she just didn't want them getting into anything and that she wasn't gone long, she just ran to get a carton of cigarettes with

Karley.  When dad came home, he yelled at Ellen and told her to stop locking the door and went and got a screwdriver and took the slide lock off the outside of the door.  I could tell Ellen was pissed off and I knew she was going to try to get back at me after this.  I always had to be on guard around her.  She was a slime ball.

I spent the summer going into 9$^{th}$ grade hanging out with friends away from the house as much as I could.  I could never bring friends home again as the state of the home was always a mix of feral children chaos, screaming and fighting kids, breaking things, and just overall turmoil.  Most nights Ellen would be gone playing bingo and I would try to be in bed before she came back.  She made me sick.  The kids were not smart and struggled in school.  They got no help at home.  Karley started stealing from the stores.  We ran up a charge tab at the gas station next to our house.  Everyone was fending for themselves.  Dad was still working when he could and Ellen was not working as much as she had a little one and it was hard enough for Karley to manage the 3 boys, now there was another baby added to the mix.

Lanny graduated and was still dating Renee. She was still in high school and was a senior at the same school where Lola was now a sophomore, and I was going into 9$^{th}$ grade.  Renee came from a good family, and they had a swimming pool.  She had a car to drive, and we went out to her house swimming.  US, not THEM.  Renee felt sorry for Ellen's little ones because she had a huge heart of gold and was the sweetest person in the whole world.  They were not well-cared for even when Ellen was home, but most times, she wasn't home.  We didn't stay in this house much longer, and by the end of the summer we were moving again.  I would say this was due to the house being torn to shreds, pissed in, windows broken, and not paying rent were probably good reasons.  Not to mention we didn't have any money for trash service, so there was a pile of garbage and garbage bags so high in the garage we could never use it. Just disgusting. This house was eventually torn down.

We moved again but stayed in Bellevue. Thankfully, I could say we have been in this town the longest. 4 full consecutive school years in one school district and going into my 5<sup>th</sup> school year in Bellevue. It was about my 10<sup>th</sup> different place to live, but at least I stayed in the same school district. And I had some friends. I spent the night at a few places. But only one time, at the country house, I had friends stay with me. Of course, we moved to a house that needed some major repairs. Half the house was closed off with holes in the floorboards where you could see outside. Sounds like a perfect place for animal children to be locked in and live in. Every time Ellen locked their room door, I would open it. She started getting pissed off and accused them of climbing out windows, which they did, and opening the door, which they didn't do. That was me. She nailed the windows shut. I hated her. I tried to reason with her as to why that was a fire hazard, and she didn't care. I asked dad to please take the lock off their door, eventually he did. She started sitting beside their door knitting and would whack them with a belt if they came out of their room. She was good and making thick and comfortable blankets out of yarn. She could create something so awesome. She would sit there for hours, rocking back and forth, knitting and smoking and beating the shit out of her kids if they opened the door. It reminded me of the days we played prison at the beach house, which was fun for us, and I have no doubt this was Ellen's form of fun. She was not good at being a mother. She was not good at talking care of her children. She was not good at being a nice person. She was not good. They literally had nothing to do but climb the walls, which they did.

We never had a phone on a regular basis. So, I never was able to call friends or talk on the phone often or give anyone my phone number.

And I never had a boyfriend. But at least at this house, we started off with a phone and we got a VCR! We loved to watch scary movies and the little ones probably had no business watching them either. We had to go to the drive-in to watch movies in the back of dad's truck. We could never afford to go to an actual movie theatre. It was really fun. The younger ones fell asleep usually. Dad tried to fall asleep driving home too.

Ellen's mom worked at the local Goodwill store so she would be able to go through things first before it was being sold. I am not sure she was supposed to do this, but she did. And I am sure she probably didn't pay for things, and if she did, it wasn't the right price. This was also where all our school clothes came from at that time. We were not getting anything new. Not even from Grandma Rose. She had gotten remarried again to a new husband and was out traveling in an RV.

One night, we rented "Nightmare on Elm Street" and us and all the little ones even watched it. In the middle of watching "Nightmare on Elm Street" our phone rang. It scared the shit out of everyone. Ellen took the call and immediately started yelling into the phone and crying. She took my dad into the bedroom to tell him some news and they came out to share it with the rest of us. Ellen's ex-husband, Lee, was shot in the back of the head by someone in the back seat of his car in Alabama. Although no one ever told us this, we all assumed it was a drug deal gone bad. There were so many lies and stories told by Ellen, I am not even sure this story is even true. Ellen's kids were told their dad was dead. They grabbed on to her leg and cried with her, although, I don't think they really understood what that meant. Since Ellen had been around, we never heard about their dad, and they never saw him. But now he was dead. I guess that was bad. Basically, they had no father, and we had no mother, and we were all stuck with each other. It was awful.

I started off 9th grade in Bellevue. And I was going to open gyms for basketball and looking forward to the upcoming tryouts.  The team had a good football season, and I loved going to the football games with my friends and being in the stands cheering for the team. I had a good group of friends by this point, and a few crushes in school, but that didn't mean anything to a life of a gypsy. I had to leave that all behind just when it seemed like we were making some progress in stability. Changing schools and friends, again.  But I guess it only makes sense that after a few short months into Freshman year, that we would move again.   But moving was the last thing I wanted to do.  Mid-school year, again.  It was exhausting to be the new person again.  At least this time I was old enough to say goodbye to my friends and let them know where I was going.  We did have a few days' notice. This time we moved out of Bellevue and about 25 miles to the South. A new town, Tiffin. I'm sure we were kicked out for not paying rent and damage done to the house.  Ellen didn't clean the house and there were too many kids and too much laundry for us kids to possibly clean up.  My dad sure wasn't much of a cleaner.  Ellen's kids were messy. Ellen didn't do laundry very often. When she did laundry, there was so much of it, it became an all-day event at the laundromat.  Ellen didn't do the dishes either.

The next house was big enough for us all.  It had 5 bedrooms, 2 bathrooms and a basement. Lanny was with us but only for a short time before he got his own place and moved back to be closer to Renee. He was working at a factory and Grandma helped him get a nice car. My dad would fall asleep in his chair and snore his ass off. The snort, roar, choke, snore was so freaking loud.  When he worked, he worked hard and was usually pretty tired. He had a bum hip and a limp from wrecking his motorcycle when he was 18. When he was tired from working, I would rub his feet. He couldn't tie his shoes because of the hip, so I tied them for him whenever I could, so he didn't have to struggle.  He liked to run the air conditioner and the house was hard nipple cold all the time.  I would clean what I could, and I would clean up after dad.  He would always have a plate of watermelon rinds, or some left over food next to his chair when he fell asleep.  My room was always clean, and that would never change.  I tried to help dad. He always seemed so old but looking back he was only 40 years old when Lanny graduated high school.  And there were 9 kids calling him dad.  I can't imagine a bigger undertaking and the sheer amount of dedication it takes to even try to raise 9 chickens, let alone 9 children. The thought just blows my mind. Granted, the upbringing was not being done well, but that he would even attempt such a feat and take on the additional kids of another woman, just astounds me to this very day.

One of the biggest changes that happened with the move to Tiffin, was that Ellen had a steady income of death benefits for her children. This would mean the kids could get new clothes for a change or maybe toys!  Maybe she would help make sure we didn't have our electric or water turned off. Maybe she would make sure the rent would be paid. Wrong. She spent those checks on herself, and her children never had shit, and she never did shit with them or for them.  She was getting $1,600 every month for her kids in death benefits and they didn't benefit in any way, shape or form.  And that is $1,600 in 1987 money! That's a lot of money.

# The Tornado

Moving in the middle of the year again did nothing academically to hurt me. My grades and work never suffered. In fact, it seemed I was ahead of the game in math and my grades continued to remain all As with an occasional B. With this change in school districts, I went from a senior high school, back to a middle school, as 9th grade in Tiffin was at a dungeon of a school, but it was a middle school. It looked like a castle, and it was very old, but cool looking. There were two middle schools, East and West. I was attending East Junior High. We were right smack dab in the middle of basketball try outs, and I had to get to that quick because I had no intention of not being in something that would take me away from the house as much as possible. I was quick to make a few friends with a cute little blonde girl with the sweetest voice, Mona. And one of her besties, Jessie. They were nice and inviting and welcoming to me trying out and being on the team. I also tended to gravitate to another girl, Leah. She was a bit of a bad girl and really wanted to bring me under her wing and show me the ropes with her and her goofy friend, Marla.

During basketball try outs and in classes it seemed like I would fit in here.  I did my best and could definitely tell I was getting faster as the years would go on. But I still was not great with dribbling to my left, and definitely wasn't the most accurate shooter on the team. But if you needed a defender to run down a break-away steal, I was your girl.  And turns out, I was good on defense.  I could also play just about any position.  I knew all the plays from the point guard position, to forward to a center.  I could play any of those positions and run any play because I memorized all the offensive plays and every out-of-bounds play from any position.  I needed to find a way to make the team, because I'll be damned if I am hanging out at home when I could be here making new friends.  I worked as hard as I could and that weekend, I was invited to come over and hang out with Leah and Marla.  Leah only lived a few blocks away, so I walked over to her house, and we hung out talking for a while and Leah's parents weren't home.  A boy came over who was interested in Leah and invited us to come with him to a party down the street with some pretty interesting characters. When we walked up to the house, it was pretty run down, and the music inside could be heard from the street.

Once inside, Leah took off with this short, greasy-haired boy and I was left on my own in a living room full of people I didn't know. The house was hot and was thick full of weed and cigarette smoke. I couldn't stand the smell. I made my way to the bathroom upstairs and heard some arguing going on down the hall when I walked out.  Leah and her greasy-haired boyfriend were arguing with a tall boy in a black leather jacket. He tried to grab Leah by the arm, and she threw his arm backwards and it flew back and broke the window.  Leah caught my eye down the hall and said, "We gotta go."  The following Monday at school everyone was talking about Leah and the broken window. Eventually, people were told that I was there too, and I became really concerned that my reputation was going to be that of parties, weed, and cigarette smoke, when I was certainly not participating in any of that. However, I had no business being there, and really had no idea what I was getting myself into, but I just played dumb and did my best to distance myself from Leah. I never wanted to have to start off with a reputation in my first few weeks of school plus it made me super nervous that it would get to the coaches, and I would be cut from the basketball team.

Walking into the gym that Monday after school to check the list for my name to see if I made the team, made me so nervous. Leah was in line in front of me and she saw her name and turned around and gave me a high five and told me I made it too. I was so happy to make the team and I stayed friends with Leah, especially with us being on the same team and in some of the same classes, but I never hung out with her outside of school anymore. I did like hanging out with Marla as she was goofy and funny and wasn't known as a party girl. During games, I was playing more than I did in 7th and 8th grade. This team wasn't nearly as good as my friends back in Bellevue, so that was probably part of it also. There were so many new, cute boys at this school, but I tried not to lose focus on the more important things, my grades.

One of our games was well attended by so many students in the 9th grade. All of the boys were in the stands watching the game and cheering loud. At one point during a time out, the group of boys in the stands started singing, "Hey, hey Mona, I wanna know, if you'll be my girl". And they went all the way down the row of every girl on the team and sang that line with each player's name. I was almost star struck when they sang my name, it almost made me giddy. It seemed that I was fitting in, and quickly finding confidence and maybe an inkling of

self-worth. Although I still felt ugly, especially when I looked at myself
and compared myself to the other girls in my class. Most of them had
braces, and makeup, and perms in their hair, and nice clothes. I still
had frizzy hair and really nothing to tame it. I didn't wear makeup
because I didn't have any. My clothes were hand me downs, and an
occasional top or sweater from Grandma. I was hoping it was possible
to find a way to be comfortable in my own skin and not compare
myself to the girls in my class who also had boobs, and I still had none!
I wanted to be happy for a change in this new place. If only home
could settle down!

On one of Ellen's finest occasions, she was being her repulsive self
and spanking the shit out of her kids. I started cussing her out behind
her back when I was in the kitchen, and she happened to walk in there
and hear me. She approached me in my face asking me to get the nerve
to say it to her face, so I did. And I never did that. I usually said things
under my breath and tried not to start fights with her, but sometimes,
I had enough, and the words came out. I told her she was a "God
damn bitch." She smacked my cup out of my hand and poked her
finger in my face, spitting as she yelled at me to where I almost gagged
because her raunchy breath smelled like rotten cigarettes and whore. I
leaned down to clean up some of the mess at the same time she pulled
a drawer open, and I rammed my face on the corner of it. It gashed a
hole right at my eyebrow and it started gushing blood. She just laughed
and called me stupid. I bruised rather easy so within a few minutes,
around the lid of my eye was bruised. Lola was also doing what she
needed to do to get out of the house and was playing basketball on the
junior varsity team. She was a beast under the basket. She was also
not coming home every night either. She would stay with friends and
tried to find sanctuary with boyfriends or anywhere but home. Lola
saw my eye a few days later and was so angry. I had already forgotten

what happened and told her I thought it was from basketball, but she knew better. She walked right out in the living room and threatened to beat Ellen's ass. Ellen told her to go ahead, and she would call the cops. In fact, she called the cops on Lola all the time.

Once basketball season was over, we rolled right into track. There weren't too many girls from East on the track team as 9th graders, but I met a few new friends who ran track from West Junior High. Makenna was a bigger girl and she did the field events. She was loud and absolutely hilarious. She had the best laugh. She was so strong and a great motivator for hard work. We had a lot of laughs and told a lot of jokes. She could always be counted on for a big laugh any day of the week. Our practices and events were all with the high school, so this was a little bit of a change. And when we went away to relay events, only a few of us were selected from the 9th grade to go, and I was one of them. It also meant I needed to leave school a little early to head out to the high school. It made me feel special. I still loved to run. I would run a track meet every day if they would let me. It was fun and I was only getting faster, and even though I was still small and skinny, I was finally getting some muscle. I got better and better at hurdles. And I was introduced to the long jump. I would try anything, and Coach Place encouraged me to do more. We had so many older girls to look up to and teach us at the high school level. I loved it. Coach Place was one of the best coaches I ever had. From the first day, you knew exactly what he wanted from a practice, and he always praised personal bests even if you aren't the best on the team. Everything he said was positive and to push growth. I loved having someone push me in a positive way. I wish he was still alive to tell him what a profound appreciation I had for him. When I saw his passing on social media a few years back, I remembered back to some of our talks and how he always encouraged me and reminded me that he sees my potential every day.  He always said, "Give me your best.  I don't ask for much." So, I did.

While I was making new friends at this new school, I was living a separate life from Lola.  She was at the high school trying to make new friends and making her own way.  At this school, they held a 9th grade prom.  I was so nervous being new that I wouldn't have anyone to go with.  I was nice to everyone and was hoping for one of the "popular" boys to ask me.  I knew some of the girls already had boyfriends the whole year so Mona and Jessie would be going with their boyfriends.  There were a few cute boys who also ran track, and I would talk to everyone and try to just put myself out there that I was hoping to be asked by someone. And someone did ask me.  It was a boy that was in a few of my classes.  I was nice to him, and he helped with some of my questions on my schoolwork, but I didn't think of him that way.  I really struggled when Bryan sent me a note asking if I had a date to the prom yet and if I didn't if I would go with him.  I didn't want to say no and hurt his feelings, but I didn't quite know how to say I only thought of him as a friend and not "that way".  I wrote a note back and told him I would just need a day or two to think about it. I don't know what came over me. Did I really think I was better than this boy who put himself out there, probably just to be nice and ask me to the prom? I didn't know how to say no. It makes my stomach sick to think of hurting someone's feelings.  He was super sweet, and very nice.

But apparently, my brain was telling me I am not interested in nice guys, from the smart group of kids. A non-athlete. Ugh, I hated myself for feeling this way inside and wasn't comfortable with the way it made me feel. I knew how it felt to be picked last and unwanted, and here I was treating someone like that.  Great! I have established at the age of 15 that I have no desire to date or say yes to prom to a nice guy! Got it. I held off just long enough that one of the boys from the popular group, one of the athletes, Victor, asked me to prom outside right when the school day ended. I was more than excited to say yes. He was also very nice, but not very smart. He was a really good wrestler, and he was Mexican, like me. Except he had more color in his skin than I did. Nonetheless, I had a date. We hadn't really talked much, but once we decided to go to prom, we did chat more during school. He was more of a friend, and I really didn't like him like that either, but I felt like I had to have a better date than the first one. God, what a shameful thought process as a teenager. I wrote Bryan a note and told him I had a date but thanked him for asking me.

We decided we would go as a group with Marla, who was asked to prom by one of Victor's best friends, Cody. Marla was so goofy and really thought Cody was super cute, and he really was. And he was also one of the fastest kids in our grade. He asked her to go as a friend because his long-time girlfriend went to school at West, and she couldn't come. So, we were just a group of friends, but I was so excited to be part of the "in" crowd. Then when it came to planning on who would drive us there, my dad suggested we ask Grandma if we could borrow her Lincoln and he would pick us all up and drive us to the prom together. It was a perfect idea and her car looked just like a limousine, so we loved showing up in style. The next hurdle to go through was what to wear. Of course, with all the kids we had, we didn't have money to buy me a prom dress. Renee offered to let me borrow one of her dresses and helped me get ready and did my hair. She was a lifesaver. I loved having a nice dress to wear and didn't care that it was borrowed. No one had to know, and no one would even care. Although I did feel quite out of the loop as most of the girls were talking about going shopping with their moms on the weekends looking for their perfect dress to wear. One of the requirements was that it did need to be a long dress. Nothing short was allowed. I felt like a princess, all dressed up.  Renee even brought me some costume jewelry to wear. She brought a pick and some mousse for my hair so that it wasn't frizzy.  Turns out, with some hair product in my hair, it is actually curly. I didn't even need a perm.

We were so young and dumb, the most important thing that night was dancing.  The couples slow danced all night, but I was more interested in the dance songs.  I wanted to get on the dance floor and dance but no one else was really dancing until they played, Mony Mony.  Marla and I got so sweaty. We danced our asses off.  I got a few dirty looks from Bryan during the night even though I made it a point to say hi to him and his friends.  I thought I did the right thing, but I guess I was supposed to say yes to the first person that asked me. I had no idea what the rules of prom are, or if that was really how it was supposed to go, but I never wanted to be put in that position ever again. And Bryan really never spoke to me again.

I had a pretty uneventful 9th grade summer heading into sopho-more year and finally back to school with Lola! I stayed home a lot and laid out in the back yard with a mirror to increase my tan.  Really all it did was give me a sunburn and increase my chances for skin cancer. I liked having a tan, but the lengths at which we had to try to get one in this Ohio weather was for the birds which is why I used a mirror to reflect the sun.  What an idiot!  I was also introduced to "sun-in with lemon juice" and "peroxide" to lighten my hair with the sun.  When I tell you how orange and red my black hair was in streaks, it makes me giggle.  But at least I was now able to get some mousse in my hair and scrunch it a little and didn't have such frizzy hair.  Lola was working over the summer and would buy some shampoo, soaps, hairspray and mousse for us to use.  We had a little bit of makeup, although I still never wore it often except mascara. I didn't really know how to put makeup on, and I wasn't interested in tips from Ellen as she caked on so much black around her eyelids and red lip stick that she looked like a street walker.  I didn't want to look like a street walker.

Over that summer I babysat a lot while dad and Ellen worked.  She was working on jobs with dad doing drywall and getting them done together as a team.  She was always most interested in coming home and cleaning up and going right back out to play bingo 3-4 nights a week.  She had to have spent $50 a night playing bingo, but there were occasions off and on when she would come home winning $400-$800.  In the long run, she thought she was winning more than she spent, but she would just sit there and smoke and blow her money on a stupid fucking gamble.  Not to mention, she didn't see her kids much or even give a shit to take care of them.  The boys were so difficult and rowdy that they were really hard to manage.  Little Joey refused to put clothes on.  Now that he was potty trained like a dog outside, he didn't want to wear clothes ever.  I would run around the house chasing him with a pair of underwear begging him to put them on.  He thought it was funny.  He would put them on his head and take off running again.  Ellen would chase him around doing the same, but when she caught him, she laid into his ass with hard spankings on his bare ass until it was all red and welted up with handprints.  He was only about 2 years old and just had no sense of structure or any hope that he would ever be normal.  One day, he was running through the kitchen, and he would pull the bread drawer open, grab a piece of bread out of the loaf, slam the drawer by thrusting it shut with his hips, and then take off running while he ate his piece of bread.  One unfortunate time, he did that while he was naked and caught the tip of his little wiener in the drawer and pinched the hell out of it.  He yanked backwards and took off running and screaming and jumped belly first onto a bean bag chair. He didn't want anyone to look at his wiener, but once dad did, he said he had a big old blood blister on it.  Poor little fella never slammed the door shut naked like that anymore.

We got two huge arcade games in our family room that someone had given to dad as a payment for one of his jobs.  Lola and her friends would have get togethers and drink when dad and Ellen were gone.  Sometimes they would take all Ellen's kids for the weekend and go camping and leave us older kids at home for a weekend.  It was the perfect occasion to have some parties.  We had loud music and arcade games and Lola, and her friends would drink.  I loved having Pac-Man and Space Invaders.  I would spend hours playing and beating high scores that the boys would set.  Sometimes they would get so mad they would unplug the game and reset everything. They didn't like to lose.  They were very competitive with video games.  So was I. Dad also did some work for a dentist and got some of his teeth fixed that were coming loose. It was nice to see him doing something for himself for a change. He started getting a big gap in the front of his teeth. He was making good money and always found a way to barter for things.  He was quite the conman.

I started up sophomore year excited to be in the same school with Lola again.  She was a literal force to be reckoned with and when people knew she was my sister, they were all of a sudden nice to me. She was dating one of the football players and we had a lot of friends in common.  She would go to parties, but I was staying home on weekends.  She would make friends with some of the kids in my grade and I started to get a little crush on one of the boys in my class.  He sat in the row beside me in my English class.  He played basketball, not football. So, he would be in the stands with us girls at the football games.  He was tall and skinny and super cute.  Overall, a very sweet guy. My girlfriends also liked having Lola in our corner, because there were some really mean seniors who liked to pick on the sophomores on a regular basis. It was a ritual, I guess or a requirement of being a senior.  To celebrate upcoming homecoming weekend, there was a bon fire held out in the country where they set a big fire and the school band played fight songs.  The cheerleaders and flag squad all came in uniform, and I loved what the flag squad did.  They wore tall, white go-go boots and 2 of our sophomore girls were on the team. During the get-together, one of the seniors noticed I was apparently standing too close to the front.  She was a short blonde with sky-high ratted bangs.  She elbowed me in the gut as I stood behind her.  Then she turned around and told me to "back the fuck up".  Unfortunately for her, I was standing beside my sister, who clotheslined her right on her ass. Her friends backed up and Lola asked if anyone else would like to say something to her sister.  They all said no, helped their friend up and left.  We laughed all night about that.

When it came time to try out for basketball, Lola decided she didn't want to play anymore.  I was disappointed as it would be the first time, we would both be playing JV and Varsity for the same school year.  She just decided she would rather work and spend time with her boyfriend. She liked being able to buy us our hairspray and not have to ask dad or Ellen for anything.  Plus, she said she really didn't like it. Our coaches were tough and tryouts sophomore year were hard.  We were really put to the test.  I was at least able to say I was one of the fastest girls out there. And I was really good at shooting foul shots. Everything else was questionable.  I still wasn't strong as a ball handler to the left and wasn't very good shooting from the field.  I didn't have any issues knowing that about myself. This time though, we were also combined with the freshmen coming over from West junior high to either make the team or be cut.  Thankfully we kept a big team and Jessie, Mona and I all made it playing JV.  We had a pretty decent season and I continued to learn more about basketball from Coach Hershey even though he was the Varsity coach. He was very smart, and I loved going over scout reports from the other teams. And this year for some reason dad started coming to my games. I loved seeing him sitting up in the stands, cheering. He always went to all of Lanny's football games, so I never understood why he didn't come to anything I did, but I was glad when he started doing it. He came alone. My guess was it was a way for him to get a chance to get away from the house himself. But I didn't care. I was happy to see him coming for a change.

One of the days over winter break I was home watching the kids and not feeling good. When Ellen decided to leave and go to bingo, I asked dad if I could just go upstairs to sleep. I had been coughing for days and I felt like I couldn't catch my breath. He asked to feel my head and said I felt warm, like I had a fever. I wasn't usually ever sick, so I just went upstairs to go to bed and skipped whatever dinner was going to be made. Ellen came home and started slamming cupboard doors and yelling because she told me to take some hamburger out of the freezer to thaw out. She said she was going to make lasagna the next day and wanted it out and in the fridge. I overheard dad telling her that I was sick and went to bed and probably just forgot. She pulled the burger out of the fridge and put it in the sink, and I heard her footsteps pounding up the stairs to my room. She pushed my door open, and the light shined into the room and on my face from the hallway light. She said, "Didn't I ask you to get the burger out of the refrigerator?" I said, "Yes, and I am sorry I forgot, I didn't feel good all day. Dad said I felt warm." I coughed a bit as I had been for a few days, and she leaned over to "feel my face" and slapped me while I was laying down and had no clue it was coming. I jumped up from bed and got in her face and started yelling in her face. She shoved me back on my bed and I got up and pushed her out my door and she backed up with so many steps, she almost fell backward down the stairs. She started thrashing around down the stairs that I tried to push her down the stairs and with her being pregnant again, she thought I did it on purpose. In my head, I said, "Say what?" How the fuck this bitch gonna be pregnant again. Oh my god, I can't with these people. And I didn't try to push her down the stairs, but now I wish I did. My voice was barely there, and it turned into a coughing fit, but I marched downstairs to make sure I told dad she was a liar. During my yelling and coughing fit and not being able to catch my breath, I felt like I needed to throw up. I ran to the closest place to barf and threw up in the sink. There was blood in my puke. My dad said, "That isn't good. I told you honey; she was sick. I don't know why you went up there starting shit with her."

Dad said he thought I needed to go to the emergency room, so I didn't get any sicker and I was going to need to get some medicine. When we got to the hospital, dad checked me in and told them what was wrong and after a few minutes they came to get me. They took my temperature, and I had a fever. When she listened to my lungs, she said they would need to get an x-ray. They said I had walking pneumonia. They came in and gave me a shot of something, and a pill of something and a liquid of something else. I had no idea what was happening. But they said I needed to rest and get my fever down. She said no basketball or school and wrote me a note. They gave dad some prescriptions and sent us on our way. This ordeal took hours. I hated every minute of it. In the car ride on the way home dad handed me the bag of everything and all of the papers and notes had Karley's name on it. He said he gave them her medical card to pay for everything or else we would have had a huge bill. I never had insurance and thankfully I was hardly ever sick, but I would have never been able to get anything medically if I needed it.

Lanny staying behind in Bellevue was the best thing for him to start his own life and get a break from the chaos. It was also nice going back to 8 in the house when he left. But we couldn't just take advantage of being down one mouth to feed. Jenna was the baby, the last of the line of kids Ellen would pop out. Jenna was born on Cinco de Mayo right at the end of my track season. She was a little stuck and needed to be suctioned out. This is a bit surprising with as many kids as Ellen had, Jenna being the 6th, that babies should just fall out of her cooter. But Jenna's head was shaped like one of the coneheads from Saturday Night Live. So that is what we called her, Conehead. She wore hats a lot. She was awfully cute with dark black hair and beautiful hazel eyes. Ellen would go around telling anyone who would listen to her that she has 11 children. Mind you, adding Jenna made 10 of us. But that skank would include my brother that died as her son. She would make us all sick. I hated it when she would tell people I was her daughter. I would think, "No bitch, no I'm not!" She has done that our whole life and tells people she has 11 kids, so people would comment at how skinny she was or give her some sort of praise that she raised so many children. Little did they know how fucking horrible of a mom she was and that she is actually a disgusting human being.

Thankfully, our house in Tiffin was only a block from the high school and town. I could walk most places, and getting to school and practices was going to be so simple for a change. In all my life, we never had a crib in the house for Joey, so it was not a surprise that Jenna wouldn't have one either. There was a laundry room that was constantly filled with laundry no one would do mainly because we never had laundry soap or sometimes didn't have water, or electric, or even a working washer or dryer. We made do with the space we had. I was sharing a room with Karley. And Lola made herself a room in the basement after Lanny moved out. Karley was not bright, and she snored. I couldn't handle the snoring, so I made her sleep on the floor. There was no way I could share a bed with her. Besides, she sometimes slept with her head propped up in her hand and her eyes were open. She was so weird. Sometimes, I would step on her when I would climb in my window at night. She was also not a clean kid. Karley had a prior broken arm and a weird-looking scar up and down it. She could have been a cute kid, but she didn't have any ambition to learn or be clean or to be anything but lazy. The boys all shared a room upstairs, which was a mattress on the floor because they would break everything. They would jump on every bed they ever had and broke everything. Then they would use the wood to beat the shit out of each other. There was a bathroom upstairs for them to piss all over. They were disgusting. When I say they broke everything, I meant, everything. Windows. Doors. Beds. Dressers. Walls. Closet rods. Lamps. Bedside tables. Chairs. Pencils. Electronics. TVs. EVERYTHING. Their room consisted of broken, torn up pieces of whatever unidentifiable anything they tore into. They were like little animals. Christian was the exception. He hated dirty, and he was definitely different than THEM. On one occasion, one of the boys set their mattress on fire! Heathens! Jenna always shared a room with Ellen and dad. She was a whiny baby and was sick a lot. She slept on a small mattress on their floor.

One night dad and Ellen went out drinking and to listen to music at one of the bars. Jenna was roasting hot and had been sick all day, but Ellen didn't care. She left anyway and told us to give her some aspirin. She was only a few months old, so Lola and I looked at each other and tried to figure out what we were supposed to give her since we had no idea much about medicine, let alone medicine for a baby. Lola thought maybe we need so smash up an aspirin and give it to Jenna on a little spoon with some of her formula. Ellen freaked out when we told her that's what we gave her after they came home. She then went in her bedroom in a drawer and pulled out a small bottle of baby Tylenol and said that was what we were supposed to give her in a dropper. Lola and I both laughed because Ellen was literally so fucking stupid, like how in the fuck were we supposed to know where to find it or even how much to give her? Literally all she said was to give her some aspirin if she felt warm, so we did just that. Ellen thought we were just fucking around and trying to hurt Jenna. We both told her not to ask us to watch her fucking kids ever again then.

During track season, dad kept showing up more and more. He would be hanging out at the fence by the finish line. As a sophomore I was placing 3rd here and there in the 100m dash, 100m hurdles, 200m dash, and long lump. Coach Place would keep track each time someone placed and how many points that would earn for the team. If you scored so many points during the school year, you would earn a Varsity letter. At the last meet of the year, we were away and against a smaller school. Coach put me in 4 events and told me I needed several different combinations of points to earn my Varsity letter and it was my last shot to do it. I basically needed to place in 2 of the events. I started off as strong as I could and placed third in all 4 events and earned a Varsity letter that year. I ran back-to-back events with the 100m dash and then the hurdles and placed 3rd in both of those. After I came across the finish line in the 100m dash with my personal best time, Coach Place was jumping up and down with his clipboard and stopwatch. He was so excited for me, more excited than I was. He jumped up and down in his blue track suit after I placed again and again. Coach said he knew I could do it and he was over the moon to see me crush my best times. He said he was going to have to promise me a letter after every track meet and show him that I have more in there. And he was right. I liked him giving me a goal to reach.

Ellen continued her tradition of going out to eat and leaving dad to make meals for the kids or fend for ourselves. She would bring home anti pasto salad from a local pizza place, and it was so good. But we weren't allowed to eat it. She wrote her name on it and "do not eat" on everything.  When she got a footlong sub, ate half and put the other half in the refrigerator, I would cut pieces off the end and wrap it back up like it was my job.  She had her name on it, fuck off Ellen.  There are 9 kids in this house, someone is going to eat this good food.  One time out of spite, I put a fly on her sub and watched her eat it in front of me.  That made me giggle and she deserved it.

One Sunday, we searched all over the house and couldn't find Joey. Ellen was freaking out and was yelling at me because I would always unlock their bedroom door.  We spread out outside and started looking down the street for him.  He was about 4 years old and NAKED! Ellen found him down the road by the very large Catholic church waving at everyone as they were walking to their cars.  When they got home, we were all cracking up laughing, but Ellen, a devout Catholic, was seething mad.  We always made fun of her for calling herself a Catholic.  I told her she was the devil of the Catholic church and to stop pretending she even knew anything about religion.  She took Joey upstairs and threw him down on the floor of the boys' room and locked the door.  I made sure to go back up there and unlock it, 5 minutes later.  She pissed me off.

At school I was continuing to excel, and my friends were talking about going to college.  That was something I never considered was an option for me but during my sophomore year, I started to actually look at different schools.  Finally, I was starting to fit in with actual friends and little crushes along the way.  I was hoping this would be our last move and my last school.  I was starting to feel confident and smart.  I never ever saw myself as pretty, and never felt it.  My friend's moms would help with hair and showed me about makeup.  I learned I had nice skin and was thankful I didn't have to battle acne like some of my friends. But I quickly learned to navigate friendships from my sports teams and friendships in school. My high school days were filled with a lot of alcohol. But while I partied on the weekends, I studied hard all week and got good grades. I also continued to participate in sports whenever possible.

Right at the end of track season, Lola, and I were going to try out for the flag squad. But neither of us would make it to try outs. We had a family tragedy, and my dad took us out of school and to Texas for over 2 weeks. We got a call that that our oldest cousin, Aunt Gail's son, Steven, had committed suicide. We packed up and drove to Texas in one day. I was so happy to be back in the sunshine and the beach. We attended the funeral, and my aunt was a mess. Evidently, Steven and his new wife, Marlita, were having problems. We were told Steven recorded a song on a tape player over and over again and left it playing in the garage and hung himself. The song was by Ozzy Osbourne and Lita Ford, "If I close my eyes forever". Evidently, he was hanging in the garage and my aunt happened to find him. I am sure it wasn't his plan to traumatize his own mother. I think he hoped his wife would find him as some sick punishment to her. However, he ended up breaking his mother's heart in two. The broken heart of a parent losing their child is something we were a little familiar with and my dad wanted to be there for his big sister.

While we were in Texas, I missed tons of schoolwork. I laid out and worked on my tan. The kids at school were saying we weren't coming back, and I am sure some of them were hoping I wasn't coming back. But in my dad's good old sweet time, we did come back. He didn't value school, and I struggled to make up the work when we returned. It was hard for me to catch on to Geometry on my own and I ended up with a C. It was the first C I ever had in my life, and I was devastated. And of course, I cried. But I got things back on track with exams and finished up the school year strong. I aced everything else and ended up with all A's and one C. Lola and I missed tryouts for flag squad for the following year, but it was fun going to practices with her and doing those dances on the beach. I would be able to try out again the next year, but with her senior year coming up, she wouldn't get another chance. And that sucked.

# Chapter Ten

# The Lightning

To complicate my calm and carefree life, I met a boy the summer going into my junior year. I had never had a serious boyfriend, just little crushes here and there, but I was still pretty shy and quite innocent. He was from the Catholic High School in town, and he was going to be a senior. He was sweet and a little awkward, and very tall. He came from a Catholic family and was a good kid. He was one of those nice boys. I was definitely a girl from the wrong side of the tracks, who drinks and sometimes smoked, and I have no doubt his parents cringed at the very sight and thought of me. I had no relationship role models. I learned about life and love on my own and screwed up at every corner I turned. I did not think about the ramifications of my actions and had very little insight to how to lead my own life in a way that would make my parents proud. My friends often thought of that, "What would my parents think if I were to get into trouble?" But I never did. I never felt anyone was proud of me for anything, except myself. I made myself proud. That also made me very selfish. And I didn't know how to treat other people. I learned that as I went also. Carl was adorable. He was kind and just adorable. I was at a graduation party with Marla, and Carl approached me to introduce himself. It was the first time my heart ever skipped a beat. It danced, and I lost my breath. My heart actually worked, whatever was left of it. I didn't know it worked and never knew that feeling for a boy, not even for one day.

I doubted I was loved by my mother. I doubted love from my father, as I was shown love very rarely. My life changed forever. My heart was so full. I didn't know what to do with that. We had friends who knew each other but we had never met. I felt an instant affection for being sought after by a boy, an older boy. I had crushes on several boys through the years, but honestly no one ever liked me back. I always felt inferior, ugly, and unattractive. I didn't wear makeup. I didn't have boobs. I chased after boys while I watched boys chase after my sister. She was the curvy one, ran with a wild crowd, and she was tan with boobs, and that wasn't me at all. He was nice and not a bad boy and every instinct in my body said, you are not his type. You are not a match. And you are most certainly not good enough for a nice boy. But Carl didn't give up. He talked all night to me and asked me to go on a date.

When he came to pick me up in a little Volkswagen, he looked too tall to get out of that car. We went to meet up with some friends of his and then went to one of my friend's house to watch a movie. He was so warm and kind. He was nice to everyone he talked to. We rented a movie, and he was just so adult in his mannerisms, and he could drive a car. That was a huge bonus. He told all kinds of stories, and we loved to just talk and hang out. He was goofy and funny, and my heart skipped beats every day I was with him, not just the first day we met. The night before school was about to start, he asked me if I wanted to wear his jersey to school so everyone would know I had a boyfriend. And I said yes, and I gladly put on his jersey to wear to school. Some of the boys in my grade made fun of me and did not like me wearing the jersey from the Catholic school at our school. They also said Carl was a dork and one of the girls in my class said he was not attractive at all. But when I looked at him, I only saw his eyes and how they looked at me. I only saw his smile and only heard the kindness of his heart. I didn't see what everyone else was telling me, and I didn't care.

I went to his football games instead of ours and wore his jacket. I loved watching him play football. He was an absolute stud. Anyone who called Carl a dork was so sadly mistaken. He was so athletic, and I loved cheering for him at the football games. I didn't hang out as much with my group of friends at my school as much as I did with Carl's friends. I liked wearing his jersey. I made a new friend who was dating one of his best friends. Mary and Drew had been dating a long time and she went to school at Mohawk. She and I became close and did a lot together as couples. Mohawk was a tiny little country school, but she did tell us all that she was coming to my school for her senior year, and I was so excited about that. Carl asked me to homecoming, and we went together. I never felt so happy in my life. After homecoming, we hung out at an after party at his parents' house and just sat around a bon fire holding hands and cuddling. His parents invited all their friends and there were a bunch of his friends there as well. He introduced me to all the adults as his girlfriend, and would say, "Isn't she so cute?" to everyone. I was so proud of him as a person and as my boyfriend. As much as my heart could know how to love a person at the age of 16, I loved Carl. My heart loved Carl. I didn't think I had much of a heart left, but I felt it beat so hard whenever I saw him. He was so tall I would stand two front porch steps up so that I could kiss him. And I would do that every chance I got.

Carl was hurt at the last home football game his senior year. He was the quarterback, and he was hit pretty hard and laid there for a while. The whole crowd groaned from both stands. But he still laid there, and he didn't get up. He never got up. And I started to panic, looking around for his parents and looking at Mary with wide eyes. I was panicking. They called for the athletic trainer, and a crowd of personnel surrounded him. I could see his legs moving, almost kicking, flailing. But I had no idea what was wrong and at that point I am in absolute tears. They called for an ambulance to the field, and he was taken off on a stretcher to the ambulance. I was scared and didn't know what to do. I cried in sadness for his pain. I felt that sorrow I hadn't known too much about while he was in the hospital. Mary was able to find out that he was taken to the hospital where he had broken ribs and a collapsed lung. She gave me the information on where they took him and the number I could call to his room. I walked a few blocks and called him on the pay phone to talk to him. It made me cry knowing I couldn't be there or see him. I sobbed most of the time on the phone asking if he was ok and if he was going to be ok. He talked in slow short breaths and said it hurt so bad, but that he would be ok. He asked his parents in the room to pick me up and bring me with them the next time they came, and they agreed. I was so happy I would be able to see him. They came and got me the next day like they said they would. They didn't talk to me the whole ride to Toledo from Tiffin which was ok because I cried the whole way there. I had a tissue in my pocket because snot and tears went together. It was dark in the back of their van, so I hoped they didn't know I was crying. They just chatted amongst themselves like I wasn't there, and I almost wish I never went. I felt awkward, unwanted, and like a burden. I know that was probably hard for them to pick me up and take me with them because I was certain they never liked me. At least I was sure they didn't like the kind of person I was or the type of home I came from. On the way to the hospital, we stopped in Bowling Green for them to drop off a tuition check to their older daughter who was in college. These parents were angels on earth, and they were wonderful parents to their large family.

When I got to Carl's room I was shaking and afraid to touch him. He looked so fragile and small in a hospital bed. He tried to lift his arm to hug me and winced in pain. His dad told him to not do anything that will hurt himself. Carl gave me a small shy side smile and tears welled up in my eyes. I could see he was hurting. We talked off and on about gossip and nothing at all, and his parents went downstairs to get some food. I gave Carl a hug and held on as long as he would let me. He wiped my face full of tears off and told me he was ok. He kept saying, "It's ok. I'm going to be ok" in short, chopped words so he could catch his breath. Carl asked if I wanted to walk down the hall with him. I asked if he was allowed, and he said of course he's allowed. We held hands and walked down the hall and visited a classmate of his that was there battling cancer. They giggled a little and talked shit for a little bit, and we went back to Carl's room. His classmate would eventually pass away as a teenager. Carl's family was very kind, very sweet people, and would never make me feel out of place on purpose. They had 5 children in their family. Carl had 2 older siblings and 2 younger siblings. His parents worked hard to give their kids a nice home, a good life, and a Catholic education. They were to be respected. This too, would be another example for me to learn from. Carl's parents came back to the room, and they had a few medical staff with them. Carl had to blow in a tube and measure how high he could blow the ball inside. And then he was asked to walk his fingers up the wall like a spider and see how high he could go. One side, he could go all the way up, but on his injured side, he winced and struggled to move it much at all.  He was told to do these exercises on a regular basis.

Carl was sent home to do some rehabilitation and would need to be cleared medically if he was going to play his senior year basketball season. He worked hard. He had great work ethic as an athlete. He pushed himself, and I liked that he was determined to get heathy and stay healthy. Basketball season rolled around, and I made the team as a junior. I played JV and Varsity.  We had a really good team of older girls who have played quite some time. But I was saddened that Mona and Jessie were cut this time around at try-outs.  They were the last of the original crew, but I was still good friends with those who stayed on from our freshman year. But there were some new sophomores who were also really good.

Carl was planning a party at his family's farm to celebrate his 18<sup>th</sup> birthday. And he wasn't cleared yet to play basketball.  This was a tradition I guess they did and a few of his friends from other schools were coming too.  They would be drinking, and I didn't hardly ever see Carl drink or ever drink around him. Plus, it was basketball season, so I didn't want to get into any trouble. The day of the party, I had a basketball game with a two-hour bus ride, 3 games (freshman, JV and Varsity) and I played in two of the games.  Then a two hour bus ride back.  I didn't sleep at all the night before as dad and Ellen were loudly fighting all night long about the kids.  I got a ride out to Carl's house after I cleaned up after I got home from basketball.  It was dark already and there were a few other people there meeting up to ride to the farm together.  While there, Carl asked me about the basketball game.  I told him that we had a bunch of girls on our team that were sick, a few were hurt, and we didn't hardly have enough players.  So, I played 3 quarters of JV and 3 quarters of Varsity.  When I went out a quarter to sit the JV game, Coach told me to go to the locker room and not to come out until the quarter was over. He said if I was sitting on the bench, he would have to put me in, and we only had 6 players for the JV game and 8 for the Varsity game. He said he would rather play with 4 players than to lose the ones he needs to step in for the Varsity time today. Fortunately, we never had to go down to 4 players, but it was an exciting and physical game. Right away, the other team was aggressive and fouling left and right. Coach also told us we couldn't get into foul trouble. However, their players did often and two of them eventually fouled out. I didn't even score any points from the field. All my points came from the foul line where I made 15/16 foul shots. Carl said that was awesome and said I missed one so I could score as many points as his jersey number. Not true, but it was cute of him to think that.

The farmhouse was only about 20 minutes away, but I fell asleep in the car ride over with Carl. I was so tired and was starting not to feel well either. I thought maybe I was getting a touch of the bug that everyone else on the team had, but it was hitting me late. Once we got there, lots of other people started showing up. They weren't just from Carl's school; some kids were from a couple of other schools. I didn't know anyone. In fact, I think I knew maybe 3 people total. Everyone was drinking, Carl was drinking, but I didn't feel like drinking any-thing. I was so tired I could feel my eyes were super heavy and I felt sore. I thought it must have been the rough two basketball games I played, but either way, I did not feel good. Apparently, this farmhouse had no heat. Carl was struggling to breathe good as the cold air was not helping with his lung issues from his prior injury. We heard some major commotion going on outside in the driveway. We ran out there to see what was going on, and some of the girls were screaming. One guy showed up drunk as hell driving like a maniac in his sports car and got into an argument with an ex-girlfriend. He said was going to shoot himself or shoot someone, and he popped the trunk of his car and pulled a shot gun out. Carl freaked out and tried talking to his friend and his friend shot the shotgun towards the corn field and told everyone he was serious. After talking him down, he handed the shot gun over, but he got in his car and left. Everyone was freaking out at what just happened. Carl took the gun and emptied the shot gun shell from it and hid it in the house.

I told Carl I was tired and needed to go lay down. Carl and I were going to sleep in one of the little rooms and I turned a little heater on to warm up in there. I told him I was going to go to sleep and bury myself under all he blankets as it was still pretty cold. While I was laying in the room off the kitchen, I could hear a couple of the girls talking to Carl. They were telling him that his girlfriend is a "piece of trash", and they were embarrassed for him bringing me around. They were saying how far down his standards are and they asked him if he knew how many people I slept with because they all heard I was a whore and screwed around. He said he didn't know and that he never asked. But that everything so far between us was completely innocent. He said we have been sorta dating for about 4 months but that we are more like best friends, that's all. He said I wasn't technically his girlfriend. Basically, I could hear him saying we are mainly friends to these girls, and I had no idea why he would say that. And I convinced myself that he was embarrassed of me. I knew this was going to happen. Again, this seemed normal for someone who hated herself for so long and for putting myself in this kind of position to have my heart stomped on. One of the guys told him that if I cared about him, I would be out there in the kitchen with him helping him with his breathing and not in the room sleeping. Again, I heard things like, "white trash" and "embarrassment" and I never heard one single word of Carl defending me. I was devastated and when he finally came in the room. I didn't even want to talk to him, let alone, kiss him. My good buddy and pal. I was going to have to pretend I didn't hear all that, because he pretended like he never said any of it, even though I heard every word. I swallowed my pride and tried to think maybe he was drunk. Maybe he didn't mean it. And I convinced myself of that, and pushed those intrusive, self-deprecating thoughts away as much as I possibly could. For as long as I possibly could.

Carl made progress with his rehabilitation, and he was practicing and playing ball again. I loved going to Carl's basketball games. As much of a stud as he was playing football, he was even better at basketball. Being 6'4" tall also helped a lot. He missed the first part of the season until he was fully cleared to play. His first game back, he was an absolute monster. He was playing in Fremont against one of their biggest rivals, and where a good buddy of his went to school, St. Joe. He broke away with a steal and dunked the ball. Carl was back. I was so proud watching him play that by the time the game was over, my cheeks were sore from smiling the whole time. Carl would also come to my games. I was so lucky to have my dad and Carl both at my games. One of our games at home, I stole an in-bounds pass under our hoop and put it right up for a score. I could hear Carl yelling in the stands, "Do it again." And I did. I stole another one and put it up for another score. Their team had to call a time out and figure out how they were going to pass the ball in-bounds. They set up a play to basically pick me off and free up their player for an open pass. I loved playing defense. I felt growing confidence in life being good, but I had started to build up the wall around my heart. I couldn't get the words out of my head; white trash, embarrassment, piece of trash, whore.

With Christmas around the corner, I was fretting about what I could possibly get for Carl that he didn't already have. But also, I didn't really have money and neither did my family. I asked my dad early on, and he said he would see what he could do to help me out.

I told him I wanted to give him a bracelet for guys with his name on it, and mine on the inside.  Like an ID bracelet that a boy would wear.  Dad said he was doing some work for a jeweler and would work something out.  And he did! I was so happy I had something substantive to give to Carl. Something he could wear all the time and think of me.  During Christmas break, Carl would stop over with his younger brother and play Nintendo with me and the kids in the living room.  We would compete for high scores. We were so goofy together and always had such a good time. He was just a simple part of my life, like a part of my family.  And I finally asked him about the comments at the farmhouse. He said he doesn't remember saying anything like that. He defended his friends, saying they were just sticking up for him. And he did want to know how many people I have slept with.  I asked him to tell me first, and he said one.  So, I said one also, even though it was zero, none, no one.  I never even thought about anything like that.  I never had a boyfriend. I never even wanted one. And in order to keep from being hurt by other people, this is why you don't have boyfriends, or give people the chance to squash your heart like a bug. I felt my heart beating hard and fast, from lying and from feeling like a liar.  But also, I don't know why I felt like I needed to embellish my reputation by lying about my self.  What. An. Absolute. Idiot! Either way, we squashed the issue and went about our business.  But, that kind of issue doesn't ever leave the back of my mind.  I would save it for a rainy day.

Carl brought my Christmas gifts over, and I gave him my box with the bracelet. He handed me a bag of presents.  I was a little overwhelmed at the sheer amount. I usually only got one thing I wanted or nothing at all. This year I got a tape player for Christmas, and I loved it. But from Carl, I got a sweater and a mock turtleneck to go underneath it from Maurice's, a pair of socks to match, a watch engraved on the back that said "Love, Carl," and the Young MC tape. I was so excited that I got a new tape player, and I played my new tape every night when I went to bed. My favorite song was "Bust a Move." To help remember the words of the songs, I would play a few seconds of the song, and write the words down, and then rewind it until I memorized every word to the song, "The Fastest Rhyme."

Carl came over for New Year's Eve. Lanny came over with Renee, Lola had a boyfriend over, dad cooked all day, and we played cards and played music, and everyone was drinking except for me and Carl. We had so much fun, and it got so late that dad said Carl could stay and I was allowed to have him stay in my room, but I had to leave the door open. So that is what we did, and we were well-behaved, and tired and literally just fell asleep listening to music and obviously kept all our clothes on. Carl lied to his parents about where he was spending the night. He parked his car down the road and came to my house. But in the wee hours of the night, Carl's dad showed up at my house. My dad came and woke us up to tell us Carl's dad was there. And usually not so soft spoken, my dad spoke softly with kindness to Carl and said "Son, you need to get down there and talk to your dad." I could hear my dad trying to tell his father we were well-behaved, and family was around but his father wasn't having any part of it. Carl was yanked down the last two steps by his ear and dragged out of the house by his very angry father. And I lived up to my name I guess as his concerned friends were telling his parents about me being trash and a whore, and I'm sure they believed it. And I made myself look like one, and basically lied about being one. Oh, the tangled webs we weave.

The next day, Carl was playing at a church youth basketball game, and I went there to see him. He couldn't hardly even look at me as his parents were there. He did his shy, side smile at me and nodded his head and waved. I waited until the game was over and tried to talk to him then, but his dad walked behind him and walked him out the door to their car. His friends that were still there said that Carl was grounded. It seemed so hilarious to me that he was 18 years old and grounded. I guess the way it looked to everyone else; it was serious, and I was white trash. And they reminded me that he has never been in trouble before I came along, and you don't just disobey your father like that. I was a little stunned at how this all sounded, but no matter how you look at it, they all felt it. The white trash whore was going to ruin the golden boy's life, and he needed to get rid of me. They also wanted to let me know that Carl had been seeing someone else, a girl from their school, and they would all prefer that the two of them were a couple. I couldn't believe what they were saying, and I think they were just trying to lie, but I was just stunned at how this was all turning out. I really didn't understand how anyone would be so judgmental to someone they don't even know. But I guess maybe I deserved it. I really didn't expect anything different.

There was always chaos in my house, at least this I was used to, and unfortunately wasn't surprised by it. I tried to get back to school after break and get my life back to normal. Back to finishing up basketball season, back to class, back to Carl, if that was even possible. The family was sitting at the table to eat. My dad made a huge pot of soup. It was boiling on the stove. Lola had a job and a boyfriend and was gone a lot. Since Dad and Ellen wouldn't buy makeup or hairspray for us, Lola would still buy me hairspray and shampoo. Ellen would hide the shampoo in the house for herself, and no one was allowed to use them, just like the subs in the refrigerator. Ellen came out of the bathroom, getting ready to go out drinking with dad, and she was spraying her hair with my Salon Selectives hairspray. I told her to give it to me and to use her own shit. She continued spraying and spraying and taunting me sarcastically like an immature child. She kept saying, "Oh, is this the hairspray you want? This hairspray right here?" Lola came around the corner and quickly stripped it from Ellen. She took the lid off and poured it down the drain and told Ellen. "You can't use our stuff I bought for us with MY money. Use your own fucking shit."

The two of them got into a literal fist fight and Ellen tried to throw the boiling pot of soup on Lola. It ended up all over the table and splattered on the floor. The kids all scattered out of there. Lola and Ellen were slipping all over the mess pushing each other around. I was just standing there in shock. Dad comes out hollering about what is going on, and just when I started to open my mouth to explain it, he backhanded me. Immediately, my eye started to swell and the ring on his hand cut my eyelid open as per usual. My favorite injury. My eye immediately started to puff up and swell shut. I had just about lost my mind in anger. Dad apologized but I didn't want to hear it. I packed up some things and went to the pay phone to call Grandma. I asked if she would come get me. After I left, Ellen called the cops and had Lola charged with domestic violence. She said Lola started the fight and threw boiling soup on her. I went to Grandma's for a few days over the weekend. She still lived in Bellevue. I cried the whole time, and I missed Carl. I asked Grandma if I could use her phone and call long distance. She said yes, for just a few, short minutes. So, I called Carl, and asked him if he would come and visit me. He said yes, and the next day he drove there to see me. He started to learn a little more about the family dysfunction as I shared with him what had happened at home, and without a doubt, if I were him, I would have run for the hills long ago. Even though my teenage heart was breaking in a million pieces, I think for him that would be the best thing for him to do.

I started drinking and running around with the girls in my class and Mary, almost every weekend and I didn't care about anyone or anything. One night with Mary, we drove to Fremont to cruise their streets and play loud music in her car. She had a really nice Camaro and we would jam the song, "Buffalo Stance" by Neneh Cherry over and over. Carl was getting tired of me showing up drunk and not knowing where I was or what I was doing. I was just living up to my reputation as white trash, and I stopped caring about anything. I stuffed my own hurt feelings down and didn't say anything to stick up for myself. I felt like I was always standing there waiting to be picked, and I was ashamed. Even though I had a boyfriend, I was alone. I always was. The only person who would have my back was myself. I couldn't see past Carl betraying me by the way he was talking about me behind my back. I used to feel like I was up on a pedestal, but after that I was just stringing myself along. My tiny, fast-beating heart shriveled up a little more that day. And I didn't think it would ever be the same. The way he used to look at me changed.

I had a lot on my plate, and I didn't have a good grip on stress. Eventually, Carl dumped me with a letter after 10 months of dating. I mean who wouldn't. I was drinking and running around trying to sabotage my whole life I suppose. I just wanted to wash his face and his eyes that used to adore me out of my brain, and just wash myself clean of him. I was broken in a million pieces. Of all the things that I overcame, of all the ache I lived through, this was almost unbearable. I sobbed for days on end. I went to school, did my schoolwork, talked to no one, came home, and sobbed. Ellen came in my room and asked me if I was going to be ok or if I was going to kill myself. I told her if anyone was going to be killed it was going to be her, and I told her to leave me the fuck alone. Forever. I was completely heartbroken for a long, long time. I left a little piece of my teenage heart and my self-worth in that farmhouse. As much as I loved, I hated. I hated him. I hated myself. I hated life. I hated people. I hated everything. I was so mad at myself for not being strong enough to stand up for myself. I hated the names people called me. I hated them for acting like they were so much better than me. When all along, the golden boy was corrupted, and I was not. I just didn't have the right kind of family or money or upbringing. I really was white trash. There were so many things I was that I should have been proud of, but I couldn't see any of that anymore. Everything changed.

I learned how to feel spiteful and anger and pain. I hoped I would never see him again and never wanted anything of his around me to remind me of him. I threw away and returned anything and everything that was from him. I saved a few pictures of him, but I hid them, so I didn't have to look at them. I tore everything else up in the smallest pieces I could. I kept the watch he gave me for Christmas but I didn't ever wear it again. Eventually, I lost it somewhere along the way. One picture I still have is of us riding around in his Volkswagen bug. The car that he actually taught me how to drive in; stick shift no less. I didn't have a car to drive or practice, let alone learn how to drive a stick shift. I carry that skill with me to this very day. I also live with the absolutely terrifying incident of being stopped at a light on a hill and not being able to get the car to go. I had to park it and Carl had to come around and move the car himself. After that, we stuck to the church parking lot for practice. The other picture is of Carl and I in my living room playing Super Mario Bros. He stopped over after basketball practice just for a little bit. He was actually perfect, and I was a shattered and a broken kid. He didn't deserve that version of me, and I should have never fooled myself into thinking I deserved him. I have tons of great memories in high school. Nothing would ever and has never come close to that first time feeling in my heart, ever. I am able to look back at the memories of those days and know just how far I came to even be in the same room as the high school quarterback, let alone that I was his girlfriend even if only for one minute. That I, a kid who came from nothing, and foster care and a shitty-ass home life was even worthy of the love of anyone.  I started to doubt anyone loved me.

I also learned bad habits and meanness as a teen.  I could dish out the most hateful and spiteful things to say to people.  I was done fucking around with trying to be a nice human being.  I wasn't afraid to speak my mind anymore and had no boundaries set for myself.  I didn't have parenting.  I didn't have the guidance of church.  I was unable to control my words, at times.  A trait I carried into the rest of my life.  I was also tired of being pushed around, tired of being hurt, tired of being taunted, tired of being smashed in my face, and I would stand up for myself from that point forward.  I didn't need my sister to do it for me anymore.  She had done it all my life but wouldn't be able to much longer once she moved out of the house too.  I zombied through the rest of my junior year, as our breakup took place over the spring right before my birthday.  I tried to concentrate during track season, but for most of the weekend invitationals, I was hung over.  And we were breaking records even while being hung over.  If I had only been more dedicated, we surely would have had a better year.  Our girl's track team ended the season for the 3$^{rd}$ year in a row as league champions.  The best part about track season was that Coach Hershey also became a race-starter, shooting the gun to start the races.  So, I got to see him all of track season, as well.  He would always chat about life and be so upbeat and encouraging.  I looked forward to seeing him at meets.  He would always find me to tell me, "Good job!"

I also became an easy target for others to make accusations that were not true, and based on my poor history, I had a difficult time defending myself.  People assumed things and I let them assume.  I was accused of following a girl at the mall and being nasty to her because Carl may have been dating her, but that never happened.  Carl called me at my job at an ice cream shop to accuse me of that. When the call came into my job from him since we didn't have a phone at home, I was hopeful it was because of other reasons and my heart skipped a beat hoping he would want to talk. I didn't know I was going to get berated about how awful of a person I am, with no ability to defend myself. That's just what I was, and eventually, what I became. I did feel betrayed by everyone. I felt that I was made out to be something I wasn't, and eventually, I didn't care what people thought anymore. I was saddened that I tried to be something I wasn't and maybe I should just stick to my own kind. We went to prom with other people, and I was just reaching out for anything, anyone who could fill that sadness and hoped he would be hurt. I also tried dating a friend of his that summer. His friend also had his own opinions of me of course, and I remember to this day he said, "Sorry to disappoint. I'm sure that wasn't as great as Carl was." And with that rude comment, he left. I was thinking to myself, honestly, that was it? That was the big fucking deal. Because to me, it wasn't a big deal. It wasn't anything to me. The girls in my class had a big game on who was still a virgin in our group. Up to that point, no one ever asked me. Everyone just assumed. I was trash; therefore, I was already a whore. So, what did it hurt at that point? I let people think the worst of me and thought about living up to it, because I thought the worst of myself.

Ever try to fix a mess you made to only make it worse with every move you made or word you said or sometimes just by the reputation you had? That was my life as I knew it at that point. I talked to Carl only one more time after that mess after a graduation party. Carl and I talked the whole night, and he cried about a few things he had going on in his life. He had a lot of stress of starting college, living up to his parents' expectations, and going on to play college sports. I was just hoping we could try something again because I was really lost without him. But I got my hopes up for nothing because that would be the last time I saw him for many years. He dropped me off at home the next morning. I watched him drive away in his little red bug and cried. I felt like I ruined my life. I would regret not ever having that feeling again from someone who I felt actually adored me, who I also adored, and no one would ever look at me the same way he did. Because from that day forward, I was no longer whole. No longer good enough. No longer innocent. And I didn't care. I stayed angry about almost everything and everyone. Instead of doing for others, I expected others to do for me. I felt I was owed something. I just assumed it was from my father, or my mother perhaps. I never realized at that age, that I owed myself something. I was a great big, giant idiot, but I thought I knew everything at that point. No one could tell me anything. I wished I could go back and tell my teenage self to respect myself before others would respect me. That would be one lesson I wish I would have been taught by a parent. I had a lot to learn for myself and find my own way and learn from the bad examples and mistakes I made along the way.

I finally got a driver's license. During the school year, I completed a driver's education course and was able to apply for a license. My dad came up with the money to get one. Jessie let me take her car for the test or else it would have never happened. There was no way I would be able to drive my dad's truck and pass the test. This little matchbox car could really zip. I had plenty of practice driving from Carl teaching me and Jessie letting me back her car up so we could unload jet skis at the lake. Dad came to get me and we drove out to the license bureau in Jessie's car from the school. The school office lady specifically said during the school day we had permission to take the test, but the extra time it took to get in line and obtain the physical driver's license card was not permitted as that could be done on the weekend outside of school hours. As soon as we walked out of the office dad said, "I'll do what I fucking want." I passed my paper test and barely passed my driving part of the test because maneuverability was hard as hell. But I passed. And we went back in with my results and got in line to get my license, just like we were told not to. It only took about 30 extra minutes. On top of that, when we were done, we drove to McDonald's to get some burgers and fries. Dad was never in a hurry to get back, and he was never on time for anything.

Every year for breakfast, Tiffin holds an academic letter breakfast. Dad liked coming to these with me because they served such good food, and it was the first time in my life I had quiche. And I liked it a lot. Dad wouldn't say much about my accomplishments, but he always made sure to find my name in the booklet. He would put his finger on my name, see what my final grade point average was, and give me a thumbs up with raised eyebrows. He would wrinkle up his forehead all the way up his bald head when he did that. It was the best "nice job" I was gonna get. Towards the end of junior year, I had one last glimmer of hope to hang my hat on. I tried out for the flag squad, and this time I made it. I was so excited to get back to my own school for football games, and what better way of being there than to be a part of our team with my friends. We partied and boy-crazied my way through the summer. Lola graduated and moved out with her boyfriend's family. One of my parties included a bunch of Lola's friends. They were playing drinking games and I was really not much of a drinker, but I was being ordered to drink up. And we were all surprised when dad and Ellen came home unexpectedly. Dad walked in the bathroom right when I started throwing up. He was not impressed. He made sure to tell me, the house better be cleaned up by the time he woke up in the morning. And it was. Also, there was another occasion that the neighbors called the cops when we were having a party and the music was up too loud. They knocked at the front door, but I just turned the music down and told everyone to be quiet, and we were not going to answer the door.  While we were all sitting in the living room, two cops came walking in and were standing over us.  They asked if a parent was there and I told them they were sleeping upstairs, but also asked the cops who let them inside the house.  They said the door was open, so they came inside because they were concerned.  One of my friends told them they are absolutely not allowed to come in someone's house uninvited, there is no need for them to be here, and she told them they needed to leave.  And they did!  We got lucky on that one.

# CHAPTER ELEVEN

# The Rainbow

That summer between junior and senior year we also had a camp at the school for flag squad to learn new routines. I had a lot to learn since it was my first year, but I was so excited to get a uniform and couldn't wait to perform on the field and on the sidelines with my friends. I loved dancing and dressing up with the team and wearing an absolute obscene amount of Aqua Net hairspray in our hair. To bond as a team, we went to the movies together and watched the movie, Ghost. We all bawled our eyes out, then went out and got drunk with the boys. I also had a job working at Heidelburg College with their food service. I worked in the cafeteria, and I worked events in the Castle on some weekends. I needed the money to survive and especially for all the alcohol we were consuming every weekend.

I came from the trashy side of life, with heartbreak and poverty. But I found friends who were direct opposites of myself, and I think that is what saved my life. I could have headed down a very different direction even though we were partying, we still had some common sense. The direction of the destiny of Ellen's kids was heading in the wrong direction. The apple falling not far from the tree was not going to be my destiny. I wanted to fall off that family tree and no longer be an apple. I wanted to be my own fucking tree!

The group of friends I had were great examples that I feel contributed to me heading down the right path in life. Hannah was smart. So smart. Straight As for as long as she could remember and ended up as our Valedictorian. She was sweet and kind and the baby of her family. She had adult siblings and didn't have a curfew. Yet, we were still in at a decent time most of the time. Her parents were older and lenient, and we partied at her house when they were gone to the Elks. Hannah's mother was so kind and sweet and was a doting mom with a soft voice and the kindest eyes I have ever seen in my life. Hannah was kind, and the Captain of our Flag Squad. As best as I could, I practiced kindness I learned from Hannah's family. Parties at Hannah's were short as we needed to be out of there by the time her parents returned. Hannah had an adult sister who would buy alcohol and accidentally leave it on her front porch for us to go by and get it.

One night, we cruised uptown, when it used to be permitted. I was in a funk of a mood with being dumped, and as we drove down the main street in town, some chic walking out of the bars yelled at us in Hannah's car. I asked Hannah to stop the car and let me out. I proceeded to walk down the street, a 17-year-old high schooler, right up to the woman who yelled at our car. And I got into a fist fight right in the middle of the damn sidewalk. We dropped to the sidewalk, and I punched this grown ass woman and the sidewalk until she wiggled out from under me and ran off. I was finding a way to make myself someone to be reckoned with and no longer be taken advantage of or hurt by anyone else. I was tired of everyone's bull shit. I was going to be the one hurting people, because fuck you.

Tara's parents were fun and funny and always fun to talk to. Tara's father was a hairdresser and her mom worked at a bank. Tara was an only child and the apple of her parents' eyes. Tara's mom made me giggle. She was sassy and beautiful and stylish. Tara and I were the most alike, which is why we butted heads the most, I guess. From Tara's family I learned to embrace humor and to laugh as loud as I could. And farting. I learned that farting is funny with Tara's family. Tara had horses and would stay the whole week at the county fair. In order for me to come stay with her, I had to sneak in with her in the truck because I surely didn't have any money to pay to get in for the week.

Mona's mom was a divorced nurse with a new lawyer husband. I talked to her lawyer stepdad about school and future goals and because of him wanted to be involved in the criminal justice system. Mona's dad was less than perfect, but she loved him just the same. From them I learned that even a broken home mends, and I also learned about strict parenting. We didn't get away with much around Mona's, but we did sneak in a time or two to skinny dip in the pool. On top of that, the liquor cabinet at Mona's house was some top shelf stuff! We would drink some and add water to it. The oldest trick in the book.

Dolly was loud and silly and adorable. She talked loudly and laughed even louder. She was a good friend to have and a great listener. Her mom was the sweetest and doted on Dolly as the proudest mama. Hannah, Dolly, Tara and I were all on the Flag Squad our senior year, and I loved it. I had another outlet to get out of the house and now I could do it all year long. Fall for Flag, winter for basketball and spring for track. I couldn't ask for anything more.

Another in our group of gals was Jessie. Jessie's father was the Junior High Principal and a drinker, but a fantastic person and a great person to talk to. He had those teacher qualities that made him easy to get along with.  He was very accepting of me even as much of a fuck up as I was.  Jessie and I had become fast friends.  I spent as much time as possible with her and she was my side kick through thick and thin. Her family went through a divorce around this time as well.  Jessie's grandmother had a house in Huron a block from the beach and a swimming pool.  We spent the rest of my junior year summer in the pool, in a bikini, and at the beach.  I felt like I was on my own and on a pretty misguided path guiding myself wherever.

My dad didn't care how long I was gone, so I was gone for days on end.  We would meet boys from the beach and ended our summer with many jet ski rides, keg parties, and boys.  One kid, Jalen, was tall and lanky with a crew cut.  I met a boy from the wrong side of the tracks, which I knew a thing or two about.  He was as bad as he was good-looking.  I never knew until later in life just how bad he would grow up to be.  He had a chiseled jaw line, and the bluest blue eyes I have ever seen.  If it was appropriate to call a boy beautiful, he was it.  He had a girlfriend or two and he was a total player.  He was a smooth talker and charming.  He could say just about anything he wanted when he looked like that.  We spent a lot of time with Jalen and his friends.  And I was at a point in my life that I didn't care much about anything or anyone anymore.  I just wanted to get this senior year out of my way and get my life started.  I ran into Jalen just one more time many years later.  He had just gotten out of prison and had a small child.  He was a drug addict.  A few months later, Jalen was dead.  He had been pulled over by law enforcement and decided to swallow a baggie of cocaine.  He ended up overdosing in the jail and being rushed to the hospital where he was pronounced dead after many hours of trying to save his life.  A tragic end for the man with the most beautiful face and eyes I have ever seen.  He battled his own demons and lost. I felt like I was always in a battle, but I never had any intentions of losing, at anything. I was too competitive for that, and I decided I was tired of being a loser so much that I hated losing.

Jessie was very much like me with a love of the beach and water. Hanging out with her at her grandma's house in Huron was perfect for us. She would load up a laundry basket full of clothes and head out for the week. And I would go with her. We had so much fun walking to the beach and spending as much time as we could by the water. We spent a lot of time in her grandma's pool also. Jessie had a lot of friends from spending a lot of time in this area and a boyfriend from Huron. He was from the wrong side of the tracks as well, but his father was in law enforcement. All of his friends were pretty shady to say the least; Jalen was one of those friends. They liked to party and have a good time and these kids had a lot of money to spend on their partying. One of those days, Jessie and I headed out to the Sandusky Mall just to kill some time during the day. When we were walking in, a yellow convertible passed us and cat-called us. We hooted and hollered back at them, and we just enjoyed having fun and getting dressed up. We laughed about those boys checking us out. When we came back out to Jessie's car, there was a note on the windshield with a phone number and an address where the boy with the yellow convertible lived. These boys were from Edison which was another school nearby and they were also loaded. We called them and set up a time to meet later that night and hung out. They invited us out on their boat and jet skis the next day. They were so cute and tan and looked so good in their swimming trunks. Jessie and I had such a good time around the beach and the water that summer. One of the boys with his blonde, spiked hair caught my eye. We became instant friends and laughed quite a bit. I enjoyed riding on his jet ski with my arms around him holding on as best I could. With us both wearing life jackets, it was a little hard to get my arms around him. He let me drive and his arms were much longer, so he was able to wrap them around me, and also take over the speed and steering when I was getting a little wild.  It was so freeing being out on the water, even if it was just Lake Erie.  The sunsets were beautiful, and it was exhilarating taking in a scene of water as far as you can see on this little jet ski.

The next day, our legs and butts were so sore from riding, when the boys asked us over again, we decided to stay on the beach.  They rode up on their jet skis and hung out with us for a little bit. They played volleyball and put on a show for all the girls to see. They were a fun group of kids.  They weren't like the Huron boys we were used to hanging out with.  We stayed friends with them all summer, but that was where it pretty much ended. We really never stayed in touch with them much after that. Oh, the joys of teenage summer loves.  Jessie still had her sights on her bad boy boyfriend and was committed to following him to the end of the earth.

I don't know what kind of trouble he was in, but Jessie and I took a trip to Washington D.C. to pick up her boyfriend.  He was staying with Jalen's grandfather. It was odd. Jessie never really told me why he was there.  He just was.  Now, I don't know who or what kind of people we were going to stay with, but Grandpa had a shotgun in his basement rafters and guns hidden all over the house.  He also had another house visitor from Paris staying in his basement. We all went to dinner including grandpa, at a Sizzler's.  I wasn't a huge fan of a buffet style restaurant, but they did have really good food. The boy from Paris and I chatted all night about music and movies and eventually fell asleep on the couch.  He had just turned 20 and was a friend of the family.  He was handsome and had the cutest accent.  He showed me his driver's license and it looked more like a passport.  The oddest thing was that it was valid for 50 years!  That was insane to me. And then we were headed back to Ohio with Jessie's boyfriend, and I was driving one of the cars back by myself so they could ride together. That was not a fun drive alone.

The start of my senior year in school, I was dating off and on and I was on a search to find myself again. I had heartache everywhere in my life. I was tired of giving a fuck and I was full of attitude. I didn't care about hurting people and didn't care about hurting myself. And since I was in school alone without Lola, I made sure things were different this time around. I wasn't taking shit from anyone, and I was saying whatever the fuck I wanted to because I just didn't fucking care about shit. Some people called that "Senioritis," but I was just fucking done. That year in high school, I floundered between trying to re-establish friendships and being alone. I drank and partied as much as I could. I never found a connection with another decent boy like Carl or any boy for that matter. I tried, but I was afraid to allow myself to let anyone close to my heart. I didn't want anyone to have my heart. I didn't even want to have a heart anymore. I think it shrunk and didn't work right anymore. I kept most relationships superficial and guarded whatever was left of my shriveled heart with a lock and key. When I felt a boy get too close, I usually did what I could to ruin things, not really knowing that I was ruining things. But when I did, I didn't even care. I wasn't going to cry anymore either.

I met another boy at the Catholic High School who was beautiful like Jalen, but he was nothing to be serious with, because he was full of himself and a player. I was more interested in his friend, Dusty. Dusty dated me, and I dated Dusty, but I tried to stay at an arm's length from him. Towards the end of the school year, we had been back and forth so many times, and I dated other boys, that I never really felt I could trust my heart to another human being. The entire football season was a blur. Flag Squad and football games consumed my life and Friday nights. We were chasing boys all around and nothing seemed to make sense.  Even though I was boy crazy, nothing stopped me from concentrating on grades. I really started thinking about what's next in life and if I have any chance at all for a future, I need to go to college.  What I had hoped for was to go to college at the University of Cincinnati and get as far away from this town as possible. Carl stayed in town and went to Heidelberg to play basketball. I thought he was an idiot for not leaving and just knowing he was going to stick around in this town made it harder to get his memory out of my brain.

My Grandma took me on a college visit to UC.  I can't believe she drove so far for me.  We stayed the night and did a whole huge visit and orientation.  She truly was the best Grandma I could ever ask for. I loved the campus. I loved their programs. I couldn't get my dad to fill out the forms I needed for financial aid.  I gave them to him over and over but he said he couldn't do them.  I didn't know it then, but it was probably because they asked for income from tax returns that he never did and financial information he just didn't have to add.

The homecoming dance was coming up and I had no idea how to feel about it.  All I could think of was homecoming last year with Carl, and my heart just didn't feel special anymore.  I didn't have or want a boyfriend, but I did still want to go to the dance like everyone else. I was hoping someone would ask me, but I literally didn't even care who because I didn't really care about anything anymore.  One boy did come to my house one night and asked me to homecoming.  Matthew was so sweet, and we have been friends the past few years.  I thought he was so cute and fun and funny, and I know I would have an absolute blast with him.  But I didn't have any affection for him.  I would rather just keep my heart to myself and complicate my life as little as possible. I went shopping for something to wear to homecoming with Jessie and I found something for $75 at the mall in Sandusky. I had some money, but not that much, so I asked if I could "hold" it and come back and pick it up once I get the rest of the money and they said yes. I had $35 in my purse, and I just needed $40 more to buy it. I could borrow shoes and anything else I needed, but this was the first time I picked out and bought an outfit of my own. I started talking to another boy in our class, one of the twins. He was also super sweet, and I did actually feel myself feeling super smitten with him. He was very handsome, and we started spending some time together in school talking. Mostly I would give him a ton of shit about how many dropped passes he had at the football game on Friday night. He was also in my art class, so we talked a lot. I didn't have any classes with Matthew, but this time around, I was going to honor the first person who asked me to homecoming and go with Matthew. Although, at the dance, I spent most of my time dancing with Ryan. I surely didn't want anything serious, so I had no intention of getting serious with anyone. Dad came through with the $40 and Jessie and I went back to the store to pick up our outfits. I was so happy.

We liked to hang out at McDonalds's after football games and the Catholic kids would hang out at Burger King. One night after a game a group of little old men got out of a car, and they were dressed so cute. I was feeling a little tipsy and of course had to make a comment to them about being so cute. Another car full of little old ladies was walking behind them, and joked around saying, "Stop flirting with our fellas." And they were cute, too. They said they had a reunion, and they were "Junior Homekids." I didn't know what that was, so I chatted with them all for a little bit about it. They all lived at a group home for kids and went to school there on the Sandusky River in Tiffin. They didn't have family and each of them called each other brother and sister. They were so bonded and close, and funny. They had to be in their 70s, each one of them. They loved their time at the Home and talked about working hard and going on to become successful adults. They get together every so often to catch up with their brothers and sisters, what was left of them. They were so interesting, and they thanked me for talking to them and said they loved telling people their stories. My girlfriends kept yelling at me over and over to come on, we were leaving, but I was so enthralled by the Junior Homekids. When I turned around from talking to these cuties, my girlfriends had left me. I found one of the football players, Jason, who was in a few of my classes and asked him if he would mind giving me a ride home. He said he was on his way out, and drove me home to my sister's house, about 3 minutes away. I thanked him for taking me home.

Before the end of the football season, one of our classmates had a party and bon fire out at his house. He had a nice house and lived a few houses down from Dolly. We all decided to go for something to do. Mark wasn't a really popular kid, but he was nice, and we were always up for a good time. Of course, we were all drinking, and I was hanging out with Ryan. At one point, another girl in our class, Lori, who was one of Tara's friends, approached me and started an argument with me in front of Ryan. She said she heard I was with her boyfriend, Jason. It took me a while to realize what she was talking about because he just gave me a ride home, and that was all. He was a nice guy and I thanked him for the ride. She said, "I bet you did. Fucking whore." At that point, Ryan kinda backed away and stared at me like I did sometime wrong. And I laughed, just laughed like a maniac. I get it. I have a reputation, and this was part of that game people liked to play. I just walked away. I went inside the house to find Mark beside himself. I asked him what was going on and he said he just wanted everyone to leave. Someone took a shit under the couch cushions in his basement, and he was feeling angry and used and sad. I went outside and told everyone Mark was wrapping up the party and wanted everyone to leave. Lori walked past me flipping me off and everyone started getting in cars to leave. Ryan ran into Jason out front and the two of them started fighting. Jason was clueless and had no idea what this was even about. Lori was yelling at him while the two of them got in his car and left. Ryan asked me if I was ready to go, and I told him to "Go fuck himself." I didn't have time for people who doubted me or didn't bother even sticking up for me, or even bother to ask me for my side of a story or input. I was just done with people and their bullshit.

At school Jason and I talked about what happened the weekend before. The two of us were just taken aback by the whole thing. I apologized for asking him for a ride and getting us into this mess, and I really didn't understand what was going on, but I didn't give a fuck. I guess I understood why people thought what they did of me and assumed things. But I had no idea how getting a ride home from someone turned into such a scandal. Well, I did understand what it could have looked like now that people are saying what they thought went on. Jason and I didn't usually talk that much but that whole week during study hall we chatted and talked the whole time. Lori broke up with him, so he was technically single now and I asked him to come over and hang out with me anytime he wanted. I figured if I was going to be accused of something I might as well check that box off for myself. I can assure you there were worse things I could do. Lori apparently didn't like me flirting with Jason and confronted me in the hallway. She walked in front of me and slapped my books out of my hands and onto the ground and said "You wanna throw?" I just opened my eyes and stared at her wild because she was dead serious trying to fight me over something that never happened and making a fool of herself looking like a maniac. I had never tried to tarnish my own school reputation and would never fight at school. I thought to myself, people are over here accusing me of being trash, but Lori's behavior was acceptable. These kids are fucked up. I bent down to pick up my books and very important school papers and one of the young, new teachers came over and helped me. He told Lori that she needed to get a move on before she got herself in trouble. She turned around and walked off after calling me every name in the book. That night Jason came over to Lola's apartment and I made sure I earned my new title of whore.

During my senior year, my dad and step-monster decided to move from the house we had in town right by the school, to a house approximately 6 miles out of town, but still within the school district. With no car, and unreliable caregivers, I dreaded the idea of living in another home in a town outside of our city. What a terrible idea. I decided I would never be able to get back and forth for basketball and decided I wasn't going to play. I was so angry at the world, at myself, and at life in general, I didn't give a shit about anyone. I got a job instead. Besides, I had a pair of basketball shoes I had been wearing for about 5 years. They were Nike and were all white. I kept them clean, but they were pretty worn out. I stewed over the move for several weeks and missed several open gyms and try-outs. Coach Hershey stopped me in the hall, and I just told him I couldn't play. My home life was a mess, and I didn't have the bandwidth to add basketball to the mix. And I needed money. He stopped me in the hall every day that week. Finally on Friday, he stopped me in the hall again, and he asked that I not say anything and just listen. He explained that life will always have its ups and downs, but that he thinks of me as his family. He said he was not going to coach next year, and this would be his last. He had tears in his eyes when he said he couldn't imagine me, one of his kids, not being on his last team ever. He told me I am special. His young daughter spent all those years and time at our practices and got to know all us girls and she was crushed that I wasn't playing. She ordered him to get me back. He said I am part of his basketball family and if

I just came back, it would mean he world to him and his daughter.  I cried, he cried, and I told him I will be there after school.  He clapped his hands together so hard and said "Fantastic. See you then." I had to stay after practices and do extra work outs to make up for what I missed. The team agreed on what that would be, and I was a sweaty mess from basketball conditioning, and then the extra work afterwards was a killer. Extra running, jump rope, foul shots, running, running, and running. It paid off and I was a starter my senior year.  It would have been a terrible mistake to not play that year.

My dad offered to buy me a new pair of shoes. He showed up at a practice with a pair of shoes in a paper bag that he had found at Goodwill.  They were not my size, and they were canvas high-top Converse and that wasn't the style at all.  I cried.  Coach helped me find a pair of shoes to wear. He helped me plan out rides to and from games and practices. One of the girls in my grade and on the team also lived in Bloomville and she would be happy to give me rides any time she can.  I was so thankful to her.  I could only think of one time that I was stuck in town with no ride home and no home phone to call to reach my dad to get me.  Dad said he would make sure someone came to get me, so I declined rides home. I was afraid to leave for fear I would miss my ride and catch hell when I got home.  However, as luck would have it, the ever-so-skanky Ellen showed up after midnight to get me after Bingo.  She "won big" and celebrated with herself with a meal and some drinks.  She was a piece of shit as a caregiver.  I was sitting in front of the school in the cold for over 4 hours.  She said "Hop in asshole" when she finally showed up and I wanted to kill her.

I think about those basketball shoes and how hard it must have been for my dad to not give me what I wanted.  It hurts my heart to know he also wanted to give me better, but there wasn't any way to do it.  If there was a way, I know he would do it. How hard it must have been to raise 4 children on his own, add 4 more on top of that, and then add 2 more.  I have a long list of ridiculous faults in my father, but it took me a really long time to realize there is a list of strengths that I carry with me in the little ways he tried and did his best.  Besides the shoes, he found a way to give me the $40 in cash that I needed for my homecoming outfit.  My emotions were in my throat and trying to choke me.  I was so grateful for everything my dad ever did for me even though some kids just come to expect it.

I really credit sports, Coach Place, and Coach Hershey for saving my life. My mentality of not giving a shit, combined with actually not giving a shit anymore was a dangerous and destructive combination to put on a 17-year-old piece of white trash. I had the opportunity to royally screw myself and my life over and would have had the time and opportunity to do it, if it hadn't been for Coach Hershey.  I was starting at forward and playing anywhere on the court, playing defense, and running up and down that court every night like my life depended on it, because it literally did. Dad came to games to cheer me on. He came to senior night and was my loudest cheerleader. We didn't go to church, but Coach Hersey would always pray with us before each game.  He bowed his head and put his hand in the middle, and so did we.  His prayer was always the same, and I felt his words in my heart.  It was one of the only real times I felt the spirit of a higher power. From Coach: "Dear Heavenly father, we thank you again for the opportunity to play this afternoon. Thank you for guiding all of our fans and parents here and please help them to get home safely. Please watch over all the players on both teams and prevent anyone from receiving any serious injuries and help heal the injuries that we do have. Lord, please help the coaches make wise and timely decisions, and help the players play their very best.  In Thy Heavenly Name, we pray. Amen." And we prayed, and I felt restored in those moments and could go out there no matter what was going on at home.  The best coaches inspire.  And I was inspired by his words and by having him as a coach for 3 years.

After basketball season, I decided to stay at my sister's apartment in town.  I could walk to school and no longer worry about being late or not picked up.  I worked before school at Heidelberg serving breakfast.  Then I would go home, shower quick and walk to school.  Then before I knew it, it was track season.  My favorite time of year.  We ended up being 4-time league champions.  These girls on our track team and I spent lots of time together.  We had a young girl who was super-fast, but she was legally blind.  We helped her time her steps and had her running hurdles.  She was awesome and so fast.  That season I became good friends with a young runner who was a state champion in cross country and track.  He was so physically fit and such a nice human being.  We even went out on a date, but we decided we were just destined to be track buddies.  I also lettered in track that season for the 3$^{rd}$ time.  I was on the leader board in several events for all the schools in our area.  And Christian was running track with me for a change.  He was fast and was winning races too.  One time, we both had our picture in the newspaper on the same day.  It was cool.  I was grossed out when my friends told me how cute he was.  Coach Place made an impact on me to clean up my life and stay involved in sports, as well.  For 4 years as a mentor, he made a profound impact on me to always give the best I have, and the rewards will come.

I got a late start nailing down plans for college.  I took my ACT and got a decent score, 26.  I was on pace to graduate in the top 10% of my class.  And I decided last minute to go ahead and apply to one college, the University of Cincinnati, and I was accepted almost immediately.  I didn't really feel this was realistically going to happen.  I didn't have any money.  I hoped secretly that my very first crush and I would be able to hang out there as he was planning to go to Xavier, which would be across town.  But fate wouldn't work in my favor, it usually never did, and I didn't have any guidance on how to make college happen.  By the time I talked to the guidance counselor about going to college, most, if not all the scholarship deadlines had expired.  She told me based on my circumstances I could have probably been able to be declared an independent student and a parent wouldn't be needed for the FAFSA.   She told me she wished I would have come to see her earlier as someone with my grade point average should be going to college.  She recommended a gap year, but to take that time to get settled financially, get a car, and get to school!  I took that to heart.  I graduated with a 3.87 GPA, and I set my sights on college.

I was still working on the weekends at the college in their halls serving for banquets and wedding receptions.  I had money to buy the things I never had before.  I went to the mall to buy my own clothes.  Before, my dad and stepmom would get us all a few things for school when they were shopping.  Sometimes we would trade each other because no one ever had what we wanted.  We never had name brand clothing unless I bought it, or I borrowed it from a friend.  And I needed to borrow a dress one more time.  Mona loaned me her prior year prom dress and I went to prom with Victor again, finishing out my senior year at Tiffin with the same person I started with at freshman prom.  We stayed good friends and were close with one another and familiar.  He was an eternal gentleman.  We partied off and on too, and he seemed to gravitate towards weed quite often, but that was never really my thing.  We went to an after-prom party and stayed up almost all night.  The next day a huge group of us went to Cedar Point and rode all the roller coasters.  Some of the crew were struggling with their hang overs. It was hilarious. We had such a good time. I felt myself drifting through the last bit of school and found it a miracle that I even made it as far as I did, with at least some of my sanity and dignity.

Right before I graduated from high school, dad decided they were going to move the family back to Texas. I never knew why, but they left abruptly and didn't give me much of a chance to figure anything out. Either I was going or not. I said no, I wanted to stay and graduate from high school from Tiffin. I didn't want to go. I was left to fend for myself for the last 6 weeks or so that were left of school. I managed to win awards and received a small scholarship from the Bloomville Lions Club with one of my last-minute applications. During the senior award ceremony, I was honored with an award for art student of the year. I loved my art class. I also received the Northern Ohio League female Scholar Athlete of the year for our school. I hadn't turned 18 yet but I was staying with Lola a lot, and now I guess I lived with her. I spent the night before my last day of school up all night drinking. I went to school with a terrible hangover still smelling like a bonfire. I still nailed all my exams. Since Dad was in Texas, he missed my high school graduation. But at least Lanny, Renee and Lola were there. As much as I didn't need him, I wanted dad there. I realized I was alone in the world for good and had to figure out life, quick. We continued to have parties at Lola's and she was just working her ass off and trying to take classes at Tiffin University. Staying with her could only be short term, and she found another place, a little bit bigger place with her boyfriend. I tagged along until graduation, but I couldn't stay with her for the long haul.

Once fall came, I moved to Bellevue with my brother and Renee and lived with Grandma Rose and her new husband at one point before I went to college. I got a job at a local fast-food place in town and saved money for a down payment on a new car. I was doing the gap year. And I was focused on making it work. Grandma's new husband co-signed for me to buy a reliable car. And finally, I had a cute little white Chevy Cavalier, and it was only a year old. I stayed in touch with my friends from high school. I visited a few on campus and checked them out to see if I would like it there too. I needed to put my life back on track. I tried to rekindle some things with Dusty after I graduated as he was just starting his senior year, but he spent most of his time drinking and smoking pot and paid very little attention to me. He was more vulgar and rude than normal. He had gone through his family splitting up and his father leaving the home. I think he had a lot on his plate that led to him being drunk all the time. I visited Ohio State, the University of Toledo, and Bowling Green State University this time around. I fell in love with BGSU.

Hannah wasn't happy with her college selection of Ohio Wesleyan University. It was her main selection as they offered to pay for most, if not all, of her schooling as she was so dang smart. Four kids in our class graduated with a 4.0 GPA, and she was one of them. We had a big class of over 250 kids graduating. Hannah told me she was considering moving to a college closer to home. Turns out it was the same college I just decided to go to. We decided to be roommates. I was so freaking excited. I applied for financial aid without the assistance of parents. I turned to the teachers from my high school for guidance, and they helped me with reference letters for scholarships and to be declared an independent student who didn't rely on parents for support. My status was accepted. I applied for any and all scholarships I could find, and I was able to use the original scholarship from the Lion's Club. I was awarded a huge scholarship from the Office of Multi-Cultural Affairs at BGSU. I didn't really have a mother, but my bloodline to her made me eligible for this scholarship since my mom was born and raised in Mexico. She didn't give me shit growing up and didn't bother getting her hands dirty raising me. But she pitched in for college behind the scenes and without even knowing. Plans for college in the fall were all set. Renee took me to do some shopping and stocked up on some things for my dorm room. I was so excited I would officially be out on my own.

Showing up on campus as a college student was a huge triumph for this white trash. Hannah and I rented loft beds and had a really cute set up in our room. Hannah was in her second year, but we were both new to the school. I loved it. My financial aid and scholarship covered everything I needed for school, including books, and I still would receive a refund check every semester for other things. My scholarship covered the meal plan, and I selected the largest one because I never wanted to ever be hungry. It could be used at the Galley food court in the basement of our dorm, a store on campus and at the restaurant in one of the halls. I was lucky. Hannah was rushing to a sorority, and I was just doing my thing. We spent our first few days running around finding out where our other classmates were living. We had a few boys from our class in the same dorm on the floor below us. One day after class, Hannah came rushing in our dorm room laughing hysterically. She said, "You are not going to believe this. Follow me, and hurry." She ran back down the hall and down the staircase. She pointed at a lady walking away from our dorm down the hall. And then she grabbed my arm, and we ran back into the dorm. I said, "Who was that?" She said, "That was Mrs. Kramer! I just saw her coming out of Brent's dorm room!" We giggled all day about that. There were rumors that Mrs. Kramer and our classmate, Brent, had crossed the line during high school, but he always denied it. She was married to another teacher and had kids! But two years after high school, there she was, visiting him in his college dorm. That sure was suspicious to us. Eventually, she got divorced and she and Brent got married and had kids of their own. These days, she would have ended up in prison!

Hannah was the best role model for school that I could have ever asked for. I was so blessed along the way to have these little twists of fate touch my life and show me what I was supposed to do. Her mom and dad were so supportive when they visited and sent her things. They even got me a Christmas present. I also got to see some tough love going on when Hannah told her parents she was going on a road trip with her sorority big sister. Her dad forbid her to do such a dangerous thing. He was so old school and told Hannah he was gonna "Kick her ass up between her shoulder blades." I could hear that through the phone across the room. Hannah still stuck up for herself and went back and forth about whether she was going to go or not, and decided to live a little, and she went! She was always able to weigh the pros and cons, made a decision and stood by it. She was a logical thinker and always had a cool head on her shoulders.

Walking through the college campus that fall with a green JanSport backpack over my shoulder, I couldn't help but soak it in. The college grounds were beautiful, but I had to get used to the wind tunnel the buildings created when walking from place to place. My hair would be whipped around in knots and on more than one occasion my umbrella was flipped inside out. I thought Chicago was the windy city! I couldn't wait to start my adult life and the opportunities were endless. I was in the best place for more knowledge and information than my little brain could possibly absorb.

Life is hard. Do you know what they say? Hurt people hurt people. But I would take that one step further, peopling hurts. We will all experience pain and trauma, but we will handle it differently. We're living in a parallel time just like everyone else. The exposures to trauma of my sister, one year older, living in the same house as me, with the same parents as me, gave her a different upbringing and childhood experience. Sometimes, it is just the way we see things, feel things, and perceive things. Sometimes, people don't try to hurt us at all. We hurt ourselves. Everyone is living in their own perception of life. They are in their own thoughts and feelings of the way life should be, how they want it to be, and what is happening around them. Sometimes we just get hurt. C'est la vie.

We could all have an opinion of who hurt who. And if we spent less time trying to point fingers at people and just remember that we are all only accountable to ourselves. Sometimes, the life we have is of our own doing. Sometimes, it's the hand we are dealt. Resilient parents raise resilient children. That is one thing that's true across the board, no matter what economic status you are. We should spend more time healing ourselves than hating people who we perceive hurt us. Their path in life may have been just as painful. More painful. Or it could have been easier based on your definition, but the level of pain and hurt they feel may be perceived by them as the worst thing in the world. You can't tell people how to feel. Spend more time giving a little grace. Spend more time worrying about yourself. Spend more time healing your inner child. Spend more time forgiving yourself, and less time hating everyone else. With a better outlook in life, we can overcome a lot of things.

My teenage heart was mending with the love I felt for myself for a change. I was thankful for every little thing. This backpack my Grandma bought me. The clothes I wore that I bought myself. This huge, thick super expensive Psychology book that my college scholarship bought me. My eyes were wide open taking in this college campus with weird looking gray squirrels running up and down the trees, chasing each other. I did it. I couldn't believe I really did it. I wrestled with the possibilities of what I wanted to be when I officially grew up! I couldn't wait to turn 21. I imagined I would get married, have kids and a dog, and a career and just be crushing it at life. It really couldn't be *that hard.* Right? After all, I had a little warrior heart. For the first time in a long time, I got picked first. I picked myself.

I will spend each day of my life loving myself, loving the path I have chosen, and in love with each mistake I have made, and my kids will make. I have a fresh start. I am proud of myself. I am April. I have completed a journey of growth. I have been all over. I have roots that didn't need to be planted. My roots come with me everywhere I go. They are connected to my ethics and integrity. I don't need to stay in one place to feel a sense of belonging. My sense of belonging comes from the value I find in myself. That was a long journey as a child with many little pieces of the puzzle helping me put that self-worth in my mind. Many teachers and other influences have shaped the kind of flower I am. I am strong. I have grown. I have weathered the storms. I survived. I did what I needed to do; April found a way to flower.

# Epilogue: Growing

Christian went with dad back to Texas, and never finished school high school, neither did Karley, Lee, Brian, Bailey, Joey or Jenna. How sad is that? Lola was living on the college campus in Tiffin and started taking classes. She was with the same boyfriend and was trying to get her own life started. She always had a few jobs and always worked to have the things she wanted. Lanny and Renee were still in Bellevue working and saving money for their wedding and their first house. The cutest thing about their wedding was Lola singing, "You Light up my Life" at their wedding. She never thought of herself as a good singer, but I thought she sounded amazing and beautiful singing from the loft of the church. She tried to hide herself, so she wasn't singing right in front of the crowd at the church, but it sounded beautiful in the church.

While working at a fast-food chain in Bellevue, I made quick friends with the crew and managers. Having been there for over a year, we knew each other pretty well and hung out outside of work too. We had a lot of fun and one of our managers would let us drink and play cards in her basement.  I was dating a boy from Bellevue, JD.  He was working for a local construction company after his graduation. During one of his work parties, the discussion about our parties with my work friends at the fast-food restaurant came up.  The company boss's wife overheard the conversation.  She had a stunned look on her face and wanted me to repeat the names of those I work with, and we had been partying with.  She became white as a ghost when I repeated Logan's name.  Turns out she knew him. Greg and his wife, Lori were wonderful, kind, and graceful people who owned a concrete company.  Lori shared a story with me, and asked that I please keep myself safe and no longer go near or anywhere with Logan ever again. A few years back, when Logan was around 16, he tried to hurt Lori. She was running around the local reservoir.  He parked his vehicle on the back side and snuck up behind her.  He knocked her down the hill and tried dragging her into the wooded area.  He had a hunting knife, rope, and a shovel in his car.  He also had a sick mind and it appeared he had intended to rape and kill her.  He was charged, but as a juvenile, he didn't stay in long, and of course was now out and about and no one really knows about that juvenile record. I never hung out with Logan again.  His name came back up a few years later.  And it is frightening to know I was in such close contact with a would-be killer in the making.  He ended up murdering a bar maid, and the eerie part of it all is that he had a hunting knife and rope in his vehicle.  He was convicted of that murder and is in prison to this day. His death sentence was overturned. You never know how many times you may have crossed paths with a future murderer. So many of us do and have in our life, and that it is scary.  In this case, I was glad to not be picked by him according to his selection standards! The thought of that, was actually frightening.

While at BG, I got a job at Fricker's. It was a new franchise restaurant that specialized in hot wings. It was a brand-new building right off I-75, and we were the first crew to ever work there. Since I was still only 19, I was hired at first as just a hostess and then was able to be trained to be a server and make more money. I did need more money to live on. I needed money for alcohol, of course. During my college stay, I got a super strange phone call. Initially, I was pissed off because it was some foreign sounding woman calling me by my nickname my dad called me, Nanny. I thought it was the girls across campus just fucking with me, so I hung up on them. However, the lady called back, and lo and behold it was my mother. She introduced herself. She indicated she had been searching and searching for us for years, trying to locate us once we became adults. She happened to call the fast-food restaurant in Bellevue where I was working to see if, by chance, someone there knew me. Of course, they all did. I worked there for over a year. I left my number and address for them to contact me or to come visit me. They gave her my number and she called. She said I shattered her heart in a million pieces when I begged her in the bathroom to take me with her. It had been almost 10 years since I last saw her running after our truck. I had only spoken to her one time in 10 years and hearing her on the phone, this strange woman, was just so odd. It took me a bit to process what adult April thought of this woman who called herself my mother.

The childhood I had was not something to literally write home about. For me, struggles became lessons I understood later. In the moment, I felt broken and beyond repair. I spent many nights of my childhood hungry, sad, cold, lonely, unloved, unlovable, unworthy, and unwanted. I laugh that I feel stronger for knowing what I know and having lived through what I have endured would crush most people. There is a quick assessment that is done on children to gauge their level of trauma. It is called ACES – and how it affects a person later in life, health and well-being. On this scale, I hit almost every single Adverse Childhood Experience. I astound myself that I can still laugh at most of what life has thrown my way.

I think we need to catch up with the rest of the family to give a real sense for where the rest of life led. Grandma Rose is no longer with us. She died in Texas. She started demonstrating some significant dementia and early on-set behaviors associated with Alzheimer's. At one point she was found locked outside of her house in her nightgown in cold weather in Ohio. She lost where she parked her car. She would misplace her purse or things and would accuse people of stealing them, including me. She wouldn't be able to recall what she had for lunch. She would say it just slipped her mind, or she would say the same thing every time. She had left a pot on the stove for hours and almost burned her house down. When on a visit with her, she would ask me several times in the span of a few minutes what classes I was taking in college. And instead of getting irritated with her continuously asking the same thing, I would give her different answers. One time I told her I was a nurse. She was the best Grandma, and my saving grace growing up. I am so thankful for every minute I was able to know her and love her. She was married at least 5 times that I could think of, and even a few old lady marriages. She made me giggle. She listened to my stories, and I loved hearing hers. She saved us in so many ways with food and money and shelter and was a soft place to land when we fell on hard times. Her whole life I felt she was taken advantage of, but inside, I know she gave her heart into helping us in every way possible.

Dad and Ellen moved back from Texas eventually. Dad worked for Lanny at his pizza shops and still had a side hustle doing drywall jobs with Ellen. He was so good at it after all these years and could do the absolute best swirls on ceilings that anyone has ever seen. Dad was a great storyteller and could talk for hours.  He had the best giggles.  He would tell us stories about stumbling across a witch in the woods in West Virginia when he was little.  And he didn't know if she saw him or not and he was trying to sneak back around to get away and she turned and pointed at him with a crooked finger.  No one knows if this was one of his tall tales or real. The stories were just good.  And he was terrible at pizza delivery. He would stop and talk to people in between deliveries or stop and get a bite to eat somewhere.  One time he delivered my pizza to me and proceeded to come on in and eat with us, helped me move some furniture around the house and just passed the time chit chatting.  When I asked him if he was off work for the night, he would say "Oh shit, I better get back!"  I didn't have much, but would love to help him if I could, knowing full well in this family no one is ever able to pay you back.  During one of his visits while he was supposed to be delivering pizza, he asked me if I would look at his foot.  He said a few days back he got scared because he noticed one of his toes was dark, almost black.  Having diabetes his whole life and battling with some weight issues, he thought this must be it.  The time has come where he would lose a toe.  He loved sweets and candy and sugar.  And it was not good for him at all.  I told him I would take a look at it not knowing what to expect.  To his right side he always struggled to get his socks off and on due to his hip issues.  So, I had to help get the sock off.  Besides his foot being a little smelly and pale, the only thing I noticed was black sock fuzz between his toes but that almost all of them were a little gray.  The socks he was wearing were black, so I asked him if they were new.  He said yes, but that since he saw his black toe, he hadn't changed his socks because he was scared. He said he took a bath and propped his leg on the side of the tub because he figured his toe was dead and he couldn't face looking at it.  I immediately started cracking up and told him to look at his discolored toes and feet. They were that way because the cheap black socks he was wearing had discolored his toes. He was so relieved, and we cracked up for a really long time about that while he should have been delivering pizzas.

Dad was a great cook for as long as I could remember. My favorites were his chili, menudo and chicken tortilla soup. One night, while dad was visiting at Lanny Jr.'s house, he fell backward and hit his head. We never were sure if it was blood sugar or if he had a stroke and then fell. When he first went to the hospital, he appeared to be functioning fine, and was sent home. Later that evening he called Lanny Jr. on the phone, and something was wrong. He couldn't get his words out and he was scrambling to try to open and take aspirin because he thought he was having a stroke. This time it was evident he had a brain injury or bleeding in his head from the fall a few hours earlier. He was life flighted to Toledo. At the hospital, he was aware, and his eyes were open, but he was unable to talk. He knew something was wrong as Lanny, Christian and I were surrounding his hospital bed awaiting transfer by helicopter. It broke my heart to see tears running down his face. He was afraid to fly. We joked that this sure wasn't the way he wanted his first flight; strapped down to a gurney. That was the last time I felt my dad looked at me with full awareness and cognition and we told him we would see him in Toledo. He went through a brain surgery due to bleeding and swelling and he had to have his head stapled pretty much back together. Ellen made a little home in the waiting room for herself with pillows and things tucked under the waiting room chairs. My dad would have never, ever wanted to be put on life support knowing his life would be a nursing home for the rest of his life. But this was the path Ellen chose for him and there was nothing we could do about it. He wasted away in the nursing home for 5 years until he died. She was doing what was best for herself as usual as this was all she ever did. She had no idea how to take care of children, let alone to take care of herself. During a talk in the hospital cafeteria, Ellen told us children that dad would want us to take care of her, give her a place to live, find her a reliable car, help her get back and forth, and whatever else she needs, like money. I think she thought we forgot over the past year she had received a lump sum retro payment of social security for not being able to work or something like that to the tune of over $20 grand. She bought one of her kids a van and blew the rest of it on shit. We all basically told her she would be given the type of care we received as children; ignored, and she could go fuck herself. We shouldn't be surprised by the audacity but couldn't believe what was coming out of her mouth.

Dad died in the nursing home in Green Springs. He eventually slowly got weaker and weaker. He was ill off and on and getting over routine illnesses was hard for him. I called him for the last time on my birthday to tell him I was going to have another baby soon. I told him it was finally going to be a boy for me. Harley was born in May, and dad died in July. He never got to see Harley or meet him. To this day that saddens me. As much as I know he did love me, and was not a great father, he did love his grandkids. He was always the favorite uncle to all of the nephews in the family. The biggest prankster. I always wonder if he watches over Harley, because I think he would get a kick out of some of the things he says and does. What has become pretty typical is usually, if they are terrible parents, they can still turn their life around and become wonderful grandparents. But I guess we will never know. My dad is buried in the plot next to my brother, Andrew. This was so painful for my mother to accept as she didn't want him in a resting place next to her baby boy she claimed dad hated. She was very angry about this for a very long time.

Ellen is still a vile piece of garbage and every single one of her kids have amounted to the same. The biggest thing I can thank her for is showing me exactly what not to do as a mother and human being. Karley ended up having two kids taken from her and placed in foster care. She also had twins she gave up for adoption privately. All 4 of Ellen's boys have been in jail and prison and on drugs. And Jenna also lost all 3 of her children and lives a life of drugs. This type of hand-out lifestyle they have led will never change and none of them have ever sought to put their life on the right path. They are all smart enough to know the right path but have corrupted their lives with crime and drugs. Needless to say, one of the most favorable things that happened with my father's death is the tie to Ellen and anything related to her had been severed for good. I never understood how my dad could live with that type of woman by his side, but he must have loved her. That's not something I have any right to judge.

Lanny is doing great. He is divorced from Renee and has two adult sons. He is the pizza shop owner. He is finally at a point in his life where he has worked so hard for everything he has that he is finally ready to accept enjoying it. He has been the most stable male-figure in my life. He has lived up to his duties as a big brother. Lola is no longer my protector and has her own 3 adult sons to protect. She is divorced and is a force to be reckoned with as usual. She is doing great working in the health care field and providing a good life for herself and her kids. Christian has moved around a lot, and never married. No kids. He is the eternal bachelor. His takeaway from our childhood is to not get too attached to anything, because it won't last. We always joke that he has a gypsy mindset. And how could you not? If we learned anything at all growing up, it was how to pack up and move on a dime.

We aren't really attached to our mother. The years of separation made us strangers and she isn't connected to us, and we don't have much of a connection to her. She found me at college, and we stayed in touch, but it wasn't a relationship with a mother like my friends had. I had plenty of supportive people filling the role of mother in my life. She could have stepped in and stepped up as an adult mom, but she wasn't much of one to us as children, we expect and receive just as much from her as an adult. Afterall, she has her replacement child to look after, and nothing has changed there in her mind or ours.

My biggest drama comes from just being a mama. I am proud of everything I have at this point in my life. Having a stable home, a stable job, and food will never be taken for granted. I find so many things to laugh about. I can't imagine life any different. I completed 4 years of college. I think of where I have been and how far I have come. Sometimes I wonder why I am who I am and why I am not something or someone else. How did my younger siblings become what they are and why are they so much different? What did they see in life that they felt they would embrace that type of lifestyle for themselves? Genetically, they belong to Ellen. The same disgusting mother raised us and influenced us. How did I choose to develop a moral compass, that was ever so lacking in my life and with others in the family? I will never know.

I still feel connected to my high school girls. I had a girl's weekend around the 30th anniversary of our high school graduation with Hannah, Dolly, Mona and Jessie. We have all grown older but realize how important each memory and bond was that we made as high school teenagers. I had the luxury of finding kindred spirits in each of them. We developed the friendships I needed at the most important part of my life when I could have headed into a very different direction. This type of friend is the one that helps you develop your heart, and they will live there forever. Those friends are the ones you literally learn with how to grow up. Their moms and dads play a part in your upbringing. Life as a teen is rough. Sharing that life with such a great group of friends is the best thing that can ever happen to a person. In all the good and bad, there are so many positive memories and fun times as a child that pale in comparison throughout the rest of your adult life. Those types of friends are the ones you can go years not seeing or having a conversation with, but once you reconnect it's like its 1990 again. Although when you are older you need those friends to help you fill in the gaps of your memory because each one of you has the rest of the story, the back story, can remember everyone's names, or remembers exactly where they were or who said what. They saved my life. And I can't begin to thank them or their families enough.

My foster mom, Dodie, just happened to be working in the labor and delivery floor when my first two daughters were born. She brought her calming force and was as close as I could think of a full circle moment when I was alone in the hospital without any support from a mother. A full circle moment I would actually want. Dodie filled some of the void in my heart of not having a mom with me or to talk me through anything about having a baby. What an amazing foster connection that by pure luck brought us together again.

I have 3 daughters who are all adults now: McKenna, Sydney, and Morgan. Harley is a teenager now! I hope my children know a different relationship with their mother. I want more. I want better. I want happiness. I fill my days looking for the silver lining. My kids will never know what it means to be hungry, or homeless, or abandoned. I like being single, and I don't have or need some man in my life who leaves piss on my toilet seat, or shit stains in his underwear, or his stiff, smelly socks on the floor. I don't have to deal with infidelity. I don't go to bed with worry, wondering where my man is or what or who he is doing. I have a perfectly full heart with the love for my children. I am not perfect. I screw up. I yell way too much for someone who is supposed to have Jesus in my heart, something my son told me when he was 5. I cuss way more than he even knows, so I would hate him to hear what I say when he is not around. I fart. I burp. And I laugh about it. I make fun of people and I like to have fun. But I work hard. I do my best and always give my best effort. That's what Coach always asked of me. I wouldn't have it any other way.

I was always able to live my life enjoying the outside, the sunshine, and the changing of the seasons. With springtime comes new life, new growth and change. With the thaw of winter, spring comes out strong, and refreshed and ready to start over. I have endured my share of winter. I have endured my share of heartache. I long for warmth. I long for sunshine. I long for dancing, laughing, singing children. I yearn for the fresh air. I feel the warm rain awaken my skin. I glow with sweat. I radiate with love and my mended heart is full of joy from my children. My soul and spirit have found peace in their eyes. A new day awakens me every morning with a chance to set my children down a path I never knew. No child should have to endure the pain of feeling worthless, unloved, and unlovable. No child should ever suffer the embarrassment of feeling less than. No child should ever be afraid to go home. No child of mine will be embarrassed of their home. They will know they are worthy and deserving of love. They will know about kindness and humor. They will know home will always be here, and so will I. They will know how proud I am of them but still expect more. I want them to do their best and give their best effort. They will endure heartache, but never be alone. They will feel in the back of their heads, "What would my mom think if I did this?" or "Would my mom be proud?" They will know about mending families and mending fences. They will know hard work and accomplishment. They will know what I know about love and life and living with a purpose. Tomorrow might be the day the sun starts shining. We will breathe in the future and breathe out the past and move forward.  I am a psychomama who loves her babies with every beat in my heart. I may have learned to grow no matter where I landed, but I will never stop reaching for something else. When life turned my flower upside down, I found a way to survive.  No matter where we are in life, young or old, we sleep under the same moon and stars and are connected by eternal love, no matter what kind of flower we are, how it grows, or who is giving us our nourishment.

For my children: Hunter, Ryley, Quincey, and Jaxx - Thank you for being the best parts of life, my soul, and my source of happiness. You have always been my happiness. I found that in you all; the happiest, most beautiful beach I could ever imagine would have you all on it.

For my sister: Maria - Thank you for being my rock and my backbone. Thank you for being my protector. Thank you for stepping up to be my best friend in the whole world. Thank you for filling in as my teenage mom and for making me the person I am today. Might be a little fucked up, but hey, we survived.

For my brothers: Larry and Morgan - Thank you for being my family and standing by me. Larry, thank you for being my carpenter and the best fixer of things.

For my dad: Thank you for devoting your life to being my dad. Thank you for being the best you knew how, for wanting to raise us kids and keep us together the best you could. You were the first to see my gifts and never stopped me from using them. I wish you were here in this life for me to say thank you for being my one true caretaker of my heart.

For Grandma Ethel: Thank you from the bottom of my heart for loving me as a child, for ice cream sundaes and Pepsi. Thank you for always saving us and literally bailing us out.

For my girls: Heidi, Monica, Jamie, Nici - Thank you for laughing with me. Thank you for showing me your hearts, the true meaning of family, and for being my kindred spirits.

For my foster parents: Dorene and Al - Thank you for giving me a glimpse at what a normal mom should look like. Thank you for saying yes to taking me and Morgan. Thank you for being super-humans who took in kids in the worst time of their lives. Foster parents should be modeled after you!

Coach Place (I wish you were here), Coach Hershey: Thank you both for saving my life. I am forever in your debt.

APRIL FLOWERS

For little girl and teenage Melanie: Thank you for believing that life is good and believing that people are good. Somehow you understood the importance of your education and thank you for allowing your teachers and coaches to be your guiding light since you didn't have one at home.  Thank you for enduring this incredible journey and finding a way to laugh along the way about life's crazy moments.  Nanny, you were always worthy of love and capable of loving.  Always remember, "A heart is not judged by how much you love; but by how much you are loved by others." – L. Frank Baum, The Wonderful Wizard of Oz.